CW00525329

20th Century
PEWTER
Art Nouveau to Modernism

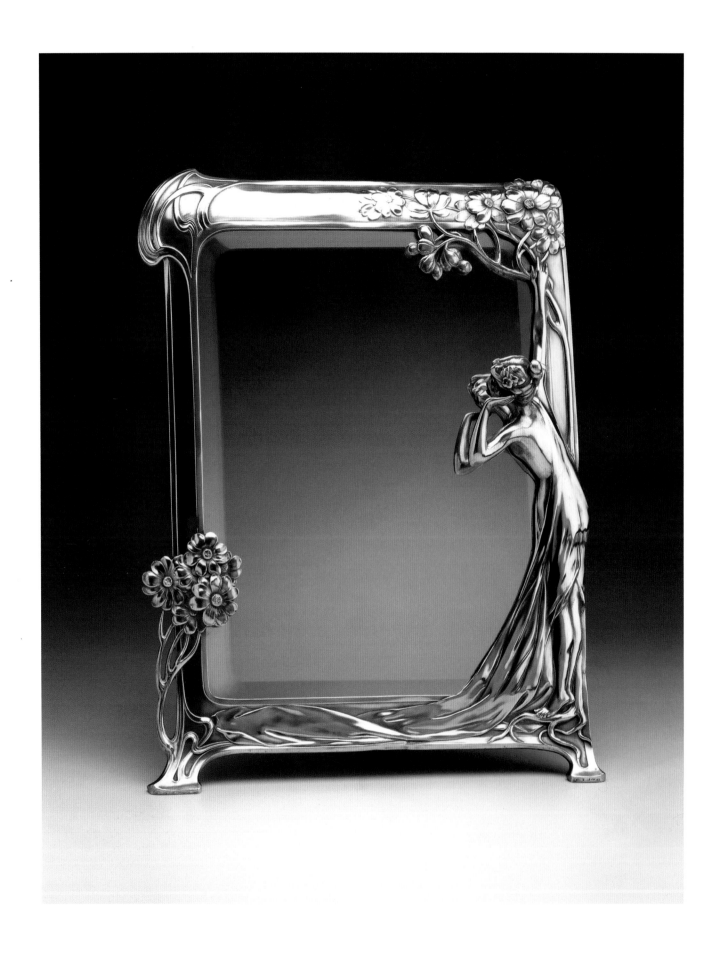

20th Century
PEWTER
Art Nouveau to Modernism

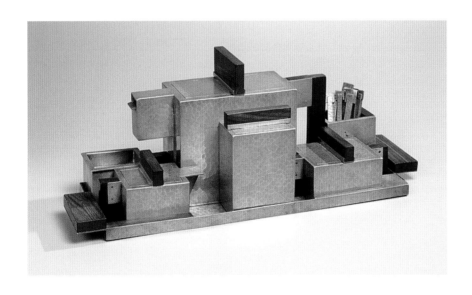

Paul Carter Robinson

ANTIQUE COLLECTORS' CLUB

© 2012 Paul Carter Robinson
World copyright reserved
First Published 2012

ISBN 978 1 85149 615 0

The right of Paul Carter Robinson to be identified as author of this work has been asserted
in accordance with the Copyright, Designs and Patents Act 1988.

All rights reserved. No part of this publication may be reproduced,
stored in a retrieval system, or transmitted in any form or by any means electronic, mechanical,
photocopying, recording or otherwise, without the prior permission of the publishers.

Endpapers: Dautzenberg/Krefeld pewter workshop c.1907. (Photo courtesy of Mr and Mrs Hoffman)

British Library Cataloguing-in-Publication Data:
A catalogue record for this book is available from the British Library.

Printed in China for
Antique Collectors' Club Ltd., Woodbridge, Suffolk, IP12 4SD

Contents

Acknowledgements

THANKS

Sara Faith Robinson
Jake Robinson
Thea Robinson
Stephen A Martin
Dody Nash
Doros Charalambides, Red Bus
  Restorations/Andrews, London
Ellis Nadler
The Pewter Society
Ann Donnelly
Alex and Patricia Neish
William Grant
The Worshipful Company of
  Pewterers
Alan Williams
Charles Hull
Professor John Donaldson
Didier and Martine Haspeslagh,
  Didier Antiques, London
John and Anna Featherstone-
  Harvey, Titus Omega
Harry Lyons
John Jesse
Paul Reeves
Sergei Glebov
Arno and Iris Bierens
Sandy Stanley
Mark Ardern

Les Hall and the late Liz Bakker
Reinhard and Monika Hoffmann
Anthony Mitchell
Galia Aytac, Abstract London
Juliet Bogaers & Alastair Nicholson
Edith Welch & the Late Stuart Cary
  Welch
Jacques Bellut
Jerry Kwiatkowski
Diana Steel
Mark Eastment
Steve Farrow
Anna Morton
Susan Wilson
Alison Hart
Susannah Hecht
Pam Henderson
Charles Gillespie
Patch Rogers, Liberty & Co.
Pablo Cal-Fernandez
Michael Strömquist, Hans Hillner,
  Bacchus Antik
Johan and Anna Karin Sjöström
Olle Sandberg, Gremeljen Antik
  Stockholm
Don Kelly Books
Cliff Usher
Carol Starr and Chalkie Davis
Steve Maris
Guy Dore

Martyn Stamp
Vera Frankl
Yvonne Jacqueline Golomb
Linda Sutton
Steve Johnson
Robert Petersen
Carol Warner
Ian Aldridge
The late Mervyn Levy
Alastair Carew-Cox
Mark Golding
Trixt Kwint and the late Jan Kwint
David and Patricia Mann
Marcus Grey
John Catto
Ralph Alfonso
Bruce D. Berry
Paul and Corinna Jackson,
  Jackson's Stockholm
Van Den Akker Antiques NYC
Paul Weatherall
Anthony Bernbaum
Marina Orpin, Valmar Antiques
Philippe Chapeau
Craig Leigh
Mark Bigler
Michael Jeffrey, Woolley & Wallis
James Strang
Wolfgang Bauer, Bel Etage
So-Nouveau Antiques

Foreword by Stephen A. Martin

At the behest of the author of this long overdue study of pewter in its myriad manifestations in the Art Nouveau and Arts and Crafts traditions, I am delighted to share a collector's perspective of this often overlooked but magical material. Until my fateful discovery of the design work of Archibald Knox, who, while working for Liberty & Co, defined British Art Nouveau and the Liberty Style, I viewed pewter as a dull and pedestrian material most associated with earlier times and limited circumstances. Little did I know that, like most casually held opinions which masquerade as truths, this one was destined to be overturned dramatically.

Knox found me in the late 1980s during the tumultuous years of a pre-recession art boom. Watching the fine art market skyrocket, both pricing me out and putting me off by the narcissism of contemporary artists, I turned for solace to decorative arts fabricated between 1890 and the First World War. What I liked about these objects was the paradox they embodied. Designed by artist-craftsmen (who were not 'art stars') to enhance daily life, they often were remarkably beautiful. This was particularly true of Archibald Knox. Living anonymously on a tiny island in the middle of the Irish Sea, he was essentially working for a department store. He would post his stunning and useable designs to Liberty & Co to be manufactured without attribution. Knox's work embodied the paradox; that is, beautiful, useful objects designed by a truly humble spirit.

My path to Knox came through pewter. Before I even knew of him and prior to actively collecting these objects, I obsessively perused books on the subject, not unlike the present one, to familiarize myself with the field. Quite by chance, I found a survey volume on the remainder shelf in my local bookstore. Flipping through it, I was transfixed by a pair of pewter designs by Knox from about 1902-1904: a buttressed bomb vase with blue green enamel plaques and a bowl with a pierced design on three supports that cradled an insert of smoky, gold threaded glass called 'Clutha'. It is hard to describe the impact on me of these two objects; they felt timeless in form and sacred in feel, like votive objects from antiquity. Yet they also felt so incredibly modern, almost 'space age', if one may use that term nowadays. Especially attractive was the soft, lustrous sheen of the surface. They felt like objects of the moonlit night, objects of the soul. Eventually, they became the first two pieces by Knox I had to own.

To this day, my unrivaled favorite object is Knox's iconic Cross Clock, inspired by, and shaped like, the standing Celtic crosses that punctuate his homeland, the Isle of Man. Constructed of flat, subtly shaped pewter sheets offset by roundels of shimmering abalone and chased Roman numerals, this large clock simply glows. Had it been made of polished silver, it would reflect away rather than invite in, emit mirrored hardness rather than seduce with gentle liquid depth. In it, this magical material transcends its humble nature by elevating a clock from being a mere timekeeper to an expression of the delicacy and evanescence of the human experience. By using pewter, a metal of deep character and changeable mood, time becomes a witness to life mutabilities rather than its master. I simply believe that Knox could not have successfully created this mystery in any other medium.

I cannot think about pewter without risking the poetic, or speaking about it in feeling terms. In the hands of many of the great designers illustrated in this book, it proves itself to be an intimate and personal material that captures the organicity of human making as it is sculpted, molded and shaped rather than hammered, bent and cut. It is high time that it now be celebrated for the remarkable treasure that it is.

Stephen A. Martin
Ardmore, Pennsylvania

Introduction

Over the last two decades 20th Century pewter has been the subject of increased interest for academics and collectors alike. Earlier European and American pewter from the 12th-19th centuries has been widely researched but little has been published about the development of pewter into the age of modernism.

By the start of the 20th century, prosperous times had created a thriving middle class and manufacturers were looking for new and inexpensive ways to mass produce upmarket domestic household items. The Arts and Crafts movement had been based on a philosophical return to the medieval guild system where craftsmanship was paramount; everything was lovingly made by hand and strictly reserved for the budgets of wealthy aesthetes. In order to make this style commercially viable, new manufacturing methods were employed. The products retained a handcrafted look, but this was simulated in the moulding and finishing.

Also at this time came the rise of the Art Nouveau style. The movement was based upon designs inspired by the paintings of the Pre-Raphaelite Brotherhood,[1] the Arts and Crafts movement, and also Japanese influences as interpreted by Christopher Dresser, William Morris, A.H.

1. The Pre-Raphaelite Brotherhood was founded in 1848 by the English painters Dante Gabriel Rossetti, John Everett Millais, William Holman Hunt, James Collinson, Frederic George Stephens and Thomas Woolner.

The Development of Pewter

Pewter is a versatile alloy which has been used to make a wide variety of household items since ancient times. It is malleable and lustrous, and was commonly used for making tableware until the 18th and 19th centuries when porcelain and glass became more popular. The main element from which pewter is made is tin (Sn) and because of this it was customarily manufactured in areas with a concentration of tin mines, such as Saxony and Bohemia in Germany, and Cornwall in the UK. Tin itself is a relatively brittle substance, so it is combined with either copper (Cu), lead (Pb), antimony (Sb) or bismuth (Bi). These other metals strengthen the tin, allowing it to be moulded into a variety of functional and alluring shapes.

Most forms of pewter that were made up until the 19th century contained lead. However, due to an increasing awareness of the harmful properties of lead, it became necessary to modify the alloy so that it would once more become acceptable for widespread domestic use. Modern pewter, or Britannia Metal as it was known in Europe, was first developed in Sheffield in the late 18th century by Ebenezer Hancock and Richard Jessop. It was composed of tin, antimony and copper, and was also given the name of Vickers White Metal.

In 1840 the first patents for silver electro plating using potassium cyanide were issued to George Elkington of Birmingham. He successfully utilised Britannia as a base metal which was then coated with a thin layer of silver or gold. When combined with the introduction of new mass production techniques, Britannia Metal transformed what was once a relatively cheap alloy by allowing it to take on the persona of a precious metal. This innovation created a cost effective way of producing luxury goods to suit most budgets. It is no coincidence that pewter re-emerged as a popular material for domestic use in Germany and England, as both of these countries had an established tradition of pewter manufacture and booming economies.

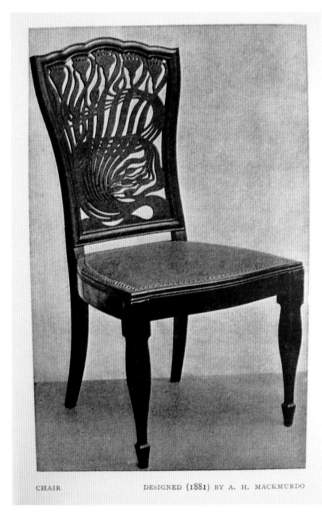

CHAIR   DESIGNED (1881) BY A. H. MACKMURDO

0.1 A Century Guild chair designed by A.H. Mackmurdo in 1881.
(Photo: *The Studio* volume 16, 1900)

Mackmurdo and Charles Rennie Mackintosh (Plates 0.1 and 0.2). Art Nouveau was an international style which infiltrated all forms of design from fine art and architecture to the decorative arts and small domestic items including pewterware. Common artistic elements included flowing whiplash lines and stylised ornamentation based upon nature and the female form.

The inspiration for the name came from L'Art Nouveau, Siegfried 'Samuel' Bing's chic Parisian shop. La Maison de l'Art Nouveau (as it was also known) created an innovative retail concept by displaying fine and applied arts in a gallery environment. The shop also included room settings in which all of the items were stylistically consistent. Bing scoured the international exhibitions for suitable goods and imported objects to fit his discerning criteria from as far away as Japan and the United States. It is likely that he was partly inspired by Morris & Co. in London and several of William Morris's designer craftsmen were retailed at this cutting edge Paris shop (Plate 0.4).

In order to celebrate the wave of optimism at the end of the 19th century, several grand trade exhibitions were

0.2 A wallpaper design by Christopher Dresser. (Photo: *The Studio*, 1900)

0.3 The shop front of Morris & Co., c.1890.

0.4 The shop front of La Maison de l'Art Nouveau c.1899.

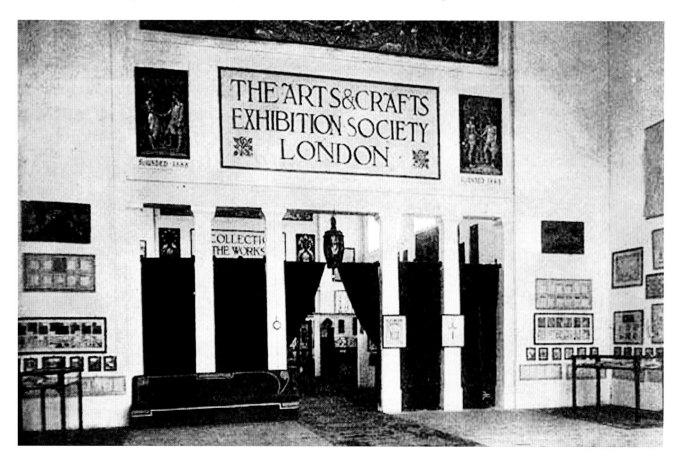

0.5 The British section of the 1902 Turin Exposition. (*The Studio*, 1902)

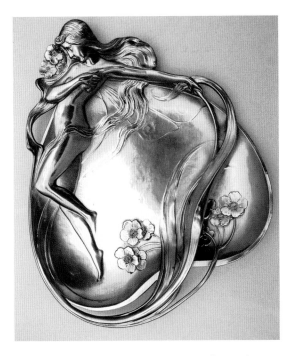

0.6 WMF pewter card tray c.1906. (FCR Gallery London)

0.7 Mucha ceramic plate 1900. (FCR Gallery London)

organised to mark the centenary. The Paris exhibition and Vienna Secession of 1900, as well as shows in Turin (1903) and St Louis (1905) were crucial factors in popularising the Art Nouveau style. These elaborate trade extravaganzas effectively globalised the movement and exposed it to a whole new generation of younger designers (Plate 0.5). Art Nouveau also received blanket

0.8 Cover of *The Studio* annual 1901. (FCR Gallery London)

0.9 Cover of *Deutsche Kunst Und Dekoration* 1902. (FCR Gallery London)

ISOLDE

0.10 Aubrey Beardsley, 'Isolde' (cromolithograph), *The Studio* issue 6, October 1895. (FCR Gallery London)

exposure in early mass circulation magazines and periodicals. The creation of dedicated art publications such as *The Studio* in England, *Deutsche Kunst und Dekoration* in Germany and *The Craftsman* in the USA was a new phenomenon. These publications frequently held competitions for designers working in all forms of the applied arts. The magazines were widely distributed and helped to spread awareness of the movement both internationally and to the provinces, with artists in Europe, America and Japan each developing their own distinctive interpretations (Plates 0.8 and 0.9).

In Germany, Art Nouveau was called Jugendstil (youth style). It possessed its own individuality and flourished at

the Darmstadt, an experimental artists' colony near Munich. The Darmstadt also contained a school within its communal structure which was founded by the influential architect Joseph Maria Olbrich. Many of the top designers of the period trained and lived in this colony and they created a wide range of pewter objects which were sold around the world and are highly sought after today.

England's contribution to Art Nouveau was a natural extension of the Arts and Crafts movement and although it remained true to its roots with the use of Celtic inspired motifs and English gothic revival detailing, the influence of the continental style is evident in many commercial items produced during this period. There were also several exceptional and original examples of Art Nouveau executed in the English vernacular style, including metalware for Liberty & Co., textile designs at the Silver Studio and illustrations by Aubrey Beardsley (Plate 0.10).

Scotland developed a completely unique approach known as the Glasgow Style. It excelled in architecture and furniture as well as textiles and metalware. In 1901 Charles Rennie Mackintosh and the other members of the Glasgow Four[2] were invited to exhibit at the Vienna Secession exhibition and strong artistic bonds were forged between the two countries as a result. Pewter was used in many of the furniture designs by Charles Rennie Mackintosh (Plate 0.11) and Ernest Archibald Taylor, whilst Margaret Macdonald utilised beaten pewter on clock faces and furniture panels. It was also intricately inlaid as an embellishment in cabinets and chairs.

Being malleable, lustrous and quite readily available, pewter was well suited to the Art Nouveau style and also to the rise of attractive goods for a worldwide market. As it was easy to care for and required less polishing than its more expensive counterpart, domestic pewter rapidly became a popular alternative to silver, with most commercial companies reserving the latter for their more traditional production. For example, it is far more common to find a neo-Georgian silver tea set from this

2. The Glasgow Four were Charles Rennie Mackintosh, Margaret MacDonald, Herbert McNair and Frances MacDonald.

0.11 Beaten lead pewter fire surround designed by C.R. Mackintosh for the Cranston Tea Rooms c.1903. (Photo: *The Studio*, 1903)

0.12 Wiener Werkstätte silver plate basket designed by Josef Hoffmann c.1905. (FCR Gallery London)

period than one in the Art Nouveau style. Designers working in pewter appear to have been given more of a free hand and many of the items seem to reflect a new found liberation and creativity.

In Germany it was common to employ well known architects and designers to work in pewter. Joseph Maria Olbrich, Albin Müller, Friederich Adler and Peter Behrens all produced artistic pewterware designs which bear their monograms. There were several small German companies working predominantly in pewter at the turn of the 20th century: Kayserzinn the firm of J.P. Kayser & Sohn in Berlin, Orivit in Cologne, Walter Scherf & Co (Osiris) and Orion in Nuremberg. All of these produced high quality items in the Art Nouveau style, but the market leader was clearly the Württembergische Metallwaren Fabric (WMF), a large commercial firm located in Wurtemberg. The WMF had the capability to mass produce pewter items and distribute the goods worldwide. Under the artistic direction of Albert Mayer the firm grasped the Art Nouveau style and successfully captured its zeitgeist. It produced a huge range of items to suit this style and the company catalogue for 1906 shows that at its peak about a quarter of the output from the factory consisted of Jugendstil designs.

The retail buyers at Liberty & Co, London's leading style emporium, were quick to pick up on the commercial

0.13 Kordofan tin chamberstick designed by Christopher Dresser for Perry, Son & Co. in 1883 and retailed through Liberty & Co.
(FCR Gallery London)

potential of German Art Nouveau pewter. They began importing these items c.1900 and soon noticed a gap in the domestic market. Liberty struck a new deal with William Hassler & Co of Birmingham, who had previously supplied the store with silver objects and jewellery, and commissioned them to produce a range of artistic pewterware. Individual designers at Liberty were not allowed to overshadow the company name, however, and as a result items were rarely signed by the artists. One exception of note was the tin or brass Kordofan chamberstick designed in 1883 by Christopher Dresser (Plate 0.13).[3] The revival of artistic pewter production at Liberty sparked a trend which was then followed by many other English manufacturers. These included some of the more traditional Sheffield companies and also William Hutton who began to produce pewter objects in both the Arts & Crafts and Art Nouveau styles.

Other countries embraced the production of pewterware in the Art Nouveau style as well. Holland had the outstanding Urania Metaal factory founded by Hubert D.F. Regout in 1903, whilst Christofle, the well known French silver/silverplate firm, also expanded to work in pewter. Its designs ranged from table items to ornamental vases with refined, if slightly restrained, decoration.

The turn of the century was, therefore, an exciting time both economically and artistically. It was a prosperous and optimistic period, and it would have been impossible to foresee the catastrophic developments of the First World War and its aftermath. These events were to bring the Art Nouveau movement to an abrupt end and would also halt the production of pewter in France, Germany and England.

3. In this case it is possible that Christopher Dresser's name was so well known that Liberty himself allowed the item to be sold with his signature stamped on the handle. Later designs attributed to him have the Perry mark and some just have a Liberty & Co. stamp.

Modernism

Modernism is a term which is used to describe the diverse range of art and architecture produced from the end of the 19th century until after the Second World War and the associated break with tradition as a result of both artistic and technological developments. It was not conceived as a style, but rather as an assorted collection of ideas, and it soon spread throughout Europe and America capturing the imagination of a new generation of thinkers. Modernism therefore encompasses a wide variety of different styles including Arts and Crafts, Art Nouveau, Wiener Werkstätte, De Stijl, Bauhaus and Art Deco. It was an experimental vehicle used to reshape and improve society; the ethos gripped and clung on, encompassing all areas of popular culture. The applied arts were especially affected by trends towards Modernism and pewter is a perfect vehicle to trace these characteristic changes.

Christopher Dresser, the Victorian botanist, is considered the father of industrial design and an early Modernist. He concluded, through his study of flora, that design was not superfluous in nature and therefore that every beautiful thing had simplicity of form and a clear function. Dresser then successfully applied these principles to his designs.

A generation later, the American architect Louis Sullivan had a similar outlook. Credited with perfecting the modern steel structured skyscraper that we take for granted today, Sullivan also had an all-embracing approach to the unification of interior and exterior design elements. In his philosophy he stated: 'It is the pervading law of all things organic and inorganic, of all things physical and metaphysical, of all things human and all things super-human, of all true manifestations of the head, of the heart, of the soul, that the life is recognizable in its expression that forms ever follows function. This is the law.'[1]

This new philosophy was also prevalent in Europe. At the turn of the 20th century, German designers Peter Behrens and Albin Müller, as well as the Austrians Otto Wagner, Joseph Maria Olbrich, Josef Hoffmann and Koloman Moser followed a similar line of thought. This core message was later taught at the Bauhaus school by Walter Gropius and Ludwig Mies van der Rohe, inspiring innovators who interpreted what was to become the international style. The French used the term Avant-Garde (advanced guard or vanguard) as the objective was to push the boundaries and create a better world.

William Morris, the leading figure in the English Arts and Crafts movement, was in many ways also a Modernist. He actively encouraged the return to handicraft guilds as a path to social reform and as a solution to the poverty which was prevalent in Victorian England. A form of social utopia such as this was something the core Modernists believed in as well, although their views stated that perfection could only be achieved through the advancement of technology. Many of the designers of the period followed these paths of thought and some combined elements of both philosophies. When the term Post Modernism came into common use in the 1970s it lead to a re-evaluation of the term Modernism and allowed the era to be put into context historically.

Stylistically, Modernism is as diverse as one would expect of a label that covers the Arts and Crafts Movement, Art Nouveau, Art Deco and post-War design. It is difficult for the untrained eye to pinpoint common denominators within its visual definition. However, one thing that links all examples of great Modernism is a shared simplicity, clarity and purity of form. In its purest form Modernism never struggles with ornamentation, as the form itself becomes the ornament and additional decoration is rendered superfluous. For example, teapots or claret jugs by Dresser, Behrens or Hoffmann are perfectly designed to balance the weight of the liquid they hold. The great masters of modern design also seize this value in their exceptional commissions for silver and pewter.

Many of the pewter designs of the Modernist period were simple and decoration was kept to a minimum. The price of silver at the turn of the 20th century was proportionately higher than it is in today's market. Pewter, however, was inexpensive and allowed for a new found flexibility. It encouraged the designer to unselfconsciously experiment with form. As a result Art Nouveau and Arts and Crafts pewter design was able to break away from the conservative preciousness which was widespread in the manufacture of traditional silver objects and it came to be used for large and opulent items designed for homes, restaurants and other public spaces. Many interior pictures of the era show pewter objects proudly displayed alongside silver and ceramic ornaments.

Following the Great War, Modernism firmly took hold in Europe and America. Its optimism captured the spirit of a world which needed to rebuild both its morale and its infrastructure. In 1925 the Exposition Internationale des Arts Décoratifs et Industriels Modernes in Paris cemented the Art Deco style through the use of highly geometric detail inspired by Egyptian, Babylonian and Aztec antiquities. From architectural finesse to the smallest everyday object, pewter was adapted for use by many of the designers working in Paris and globally. It was favoured as an inlay in decorative panels, furniture and also in vases and bowls know as Dinanderie.

The most significant pewter production of this period came from Scandinavia, although fine examples of pewter were also manufactured in England, Holland and Germany. Japan produced antimony ware inspired by Hagenauer[2] and companies in the US adapted designs to the popular Art Deco Style. Motifs inspired by Streamline and the machine age were used in much of the pewter output of this period.

1. Sullivan, Louis, 'The Tall Office Building Artistically Considered', published in *Lippincott's* magazine, March 1896

2. Hagenauer was an Austrian factory producing items in the style of the Wiener Werkstätte. They created a number of inspired boxes and bronze sculptures incorporating figures and animals into their designs.

GERMAN PEWTER

Württembergische Metallwarenfabrik (WMF)
1853 – Present

Between 1895 and 1910 the German metalware firm Württembergische Metallwarenfabrik (WMF) dominated the production of artistic domestic metalware in Europe.

Founded in 1853 by Daniel Straub, the entrepreneurial son of a wealthy miller,[1] the original factory was situated in Geislingen under the name of Metallwarenfabrik Straub & Schweizer. In 1880 it then merged with another German company to become WMF.

Their original metalware was limited to traditional designs, many of which were based on English pattern books. Production methods varied from moulding and assembling the pewter to stamping and die-casting; all items were finished by hand. WMF fervently invested in new industrial technology and quickly became the market leader both domestically and abroad. They quickly expanded production and by the early part of the new century the company had swallowed up many of the smaller Britannia metal factories in Germany, Austria and Poland. The workforce grew from 16 people when the company was started, to over 6,000 by 1914.[2]

In 1868 Straub opened his first retail outlet in Berlin. It was an immediate success and provided the model for a marketing strategy which was to be replicated in other German cities and eventually throughout the Continent. They also produced a successful series of metalware catalogues which were widely distributed.

In the later part of the 19th century demand for artistic metalware was at its peak. WMF shifted much of its production to pewter and hired the sculptor Albert Mayer as Artistic Director. The factory had already employed the notable sculptor/designer Hans Peter who is credited for crafting their earliest Jugendstil designs.[3] It is also recorded that Peter Behrens and Albin Müller, the well known Darmstadt designers, produced work for WMF during this period. Their stylistic approach to metalware production helped formulate the successful WMF modernist approach to design for many years to come (Plates 1.1 and 1.2).[4]

WMF were innovative market leaders. They captured the public's imagination and conveyed the Art Nouveau and Secessionist styles to the masses. The designs were sometimes ingenious and at other times bordering on the kitsch. They were a jack of all styles, creating a vast range of items for the home with something to appeal to all levels of taste.

WMF was first and foremost a commercial enterprise, perhaps Europe's largest. They created a enormous range of objects for the table including elaborate decanters and wine paraphernalia as well as exquisite table centrepieces, which incorporated finely etched crystal surrounded by intricate pewter mounts. Luxurious items for ladies' dressing tables were also produced, including mirrors with flowing maidens, jewel boxes and trays modelled into the shapes of fairies and frogs. For the gentlemen there were sophisticated items for desks and smokers' accessories; ink stands, cigar lighters and cutters portrayed subjects such as the newly invented automobile, bobsleighs and erotic maidens.

1. International Directory of Company Histories, Volume 60 (1989) by Evelyn Hauser
2. Art Nouveau Domestic Metalwork from Württembergische Metallwarenfabrik: The English Catalogue 1906, Antique Collectors' Club, 1988, p. ix
3. Ibid, pp. xxii–xxiii
4. It is documented that Peter Behrens produced a mirror design for A.K.& Cie exhibited at the Turin Exhibition in 1902 (Die Kunstler der Mathildenhohe, Mathildenhohe Band 4, 1977 p. 16). Albin Müller is also mentioned as a designer for WMF (Art Nouveau Domestic Metalwork from Württembergische Metallwarenfabrik: The English Catalogue 1906, Antique Collectors' Club, 1988, p. xxxiii).

There were five main styles produced by WMF:

High Art Nouveau: flowing maidens derived from Alfons Mucha are incorporated into many of the designs (Plate 1.35)

Sinuous Floral: an Art Nouveau style that uses whiplash detailing (Plate 1.25)

Secessionist: a style deriving much of its inspiration, severe modernist lines and decoration from the Darmstadt and Wiener Werkstätte (Plate 1.7)

Eclectic: a classical revival mixing Art Nouveau and Rococo with Greco-Roman detailing (Plate 1.82)

Traditional: Sheffield-inspired designs, many based on English pattern books of the 19th century (Plate 1.32)

Therefore, WMF produced a small but significant output of memorable designs in the Jugendstil tradition, notably integrating whimsical animals and sensuous women into useful items for the home. Their styles had a lasting appeal and designs by WMF are now among the most sought after pewter of the period.

1.1 WMF Secessionist pewter bottle stand (model 15) designed by Albin Müller c.1906, d. 9cm. (FCR Gallery London)

1.2 WMF Secessionist pewter bottle stand (model 345) designed in the style of Peter Behrens c.1906, d. 9.2cm. (FCR Gallery London)

1.3 WMF eclectic pewter bottle stand (model 345) designed c.1904, d. 9cm. (FCR Gallery London)

1.4 WMF Art Nouveau pewter bottle stand (model 15) designed by Albert Mayer c.1906 d. 9cm. (FCR Gallery London))

1.5 WMF Art Nouveau pewter and glass claret jug (model 190) designed by Albert Mayer c.1906, h. 41.5cm. (FCR Gallery London)

1.6 WMF Art Nouveau pewter and cut crystal liqueur set (model 190/6) designed c.1906 d. 9cm. (Titus Omega)

1.7 WMF Secessionist pewter and brass fruit stand (model 184) in the style of Peter Behrens c.1906, h. 27cm. (FCR Gallery London)

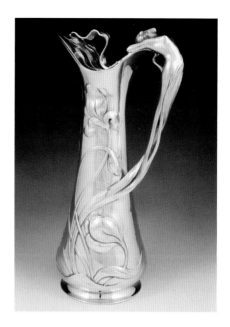

1.8 WMF pewter claret jug with Alfons Mucha style maiden c.1908, h. 41cm. (Titus Omega)

1.9 WMF Secessionist pewter wine jug (model 144) designed c.1906, h. 37cm. (Titus Omega)

1.10 WMF Art Nouveau pewter wine ewer (model 138) designed by Albert Mayer c.1906, h. 37.5cm. (Titus Omega)

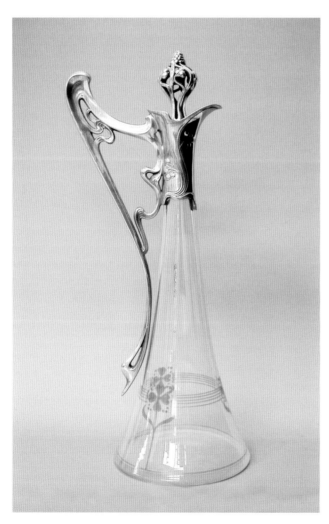

1.12 WMF Secessionist pewter toilet mirror designed by Albert Mayer c.1905, h. 77cm. (Photo: Jerry Kwiatkowski)

1.11 WMF Art Nouveau pewter and enamelled glass claret jug (model 124) designed c.1906, h. 36 cm. (FCR Gallery London)

1.13 WMF Art Nouveau pewter toilet mirror (model 131) designed by Albert Mayer c.1906, h. 37.5cm. (FCR Gallery London)

1.14 WMF Art Nouveau pewter toilet mirror (model 108/a) designed by Albert Mayer c.1906, h. 51.5cm. (Titus Omega)

1.15 WMF Pair of Art Nouveau pewter photo frames (model 18 and 18a) designed by Albert Mayer c.1906, h. 25cm. (Titus Omega)

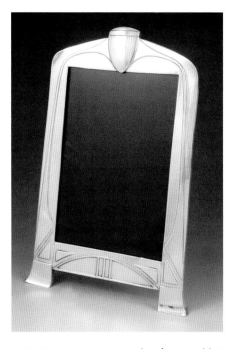

1.16 WMF Secessionist pewter photo frame (model 9) designed c.1906, h. 22.5cm. (Titus Omega)

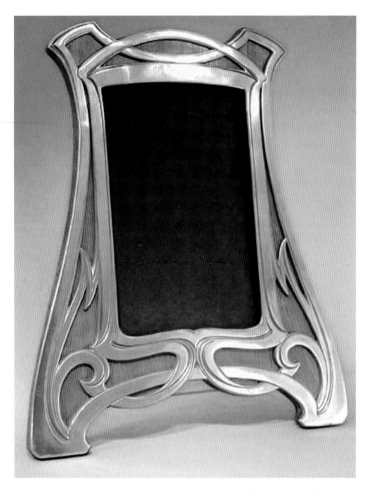

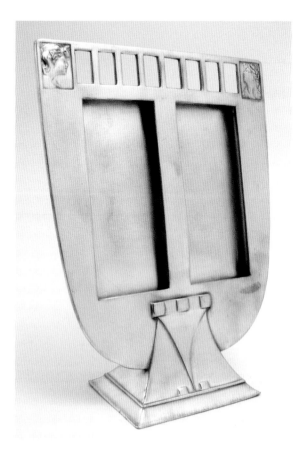

1.17 WMF Secessionist pewter 'Princess' photo frame (model 91/2) designed c.1906, h. 20cm. (Titus Omega)

1.18 WMF Secessionist pewter and oak photo frame designed c.1908, h. 22.5cm. (FCR Gallery London)

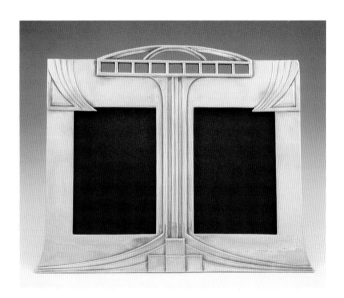

1.19 WMF Secessionist pewter photo frame (model 93/a) designed c.1906, h. 16cm. (Titus Omega)

1.20 WMF Secessionist pewter photo frame (model 92/a) designed c.1906, w. 25.5cm. (Titus Omega)

1.21 WMF Art Nouveau pewter 'Promenade' photo frame (model 132) designed c.1906, h. 22.5cm. (Titus Omega)

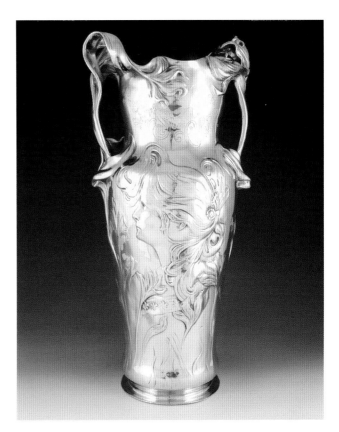

1.22 WMF Art Nouveau crystal-lined pewter flower vase (model 257) designed c.1906, h. 43.5cm. (Titus Omega)

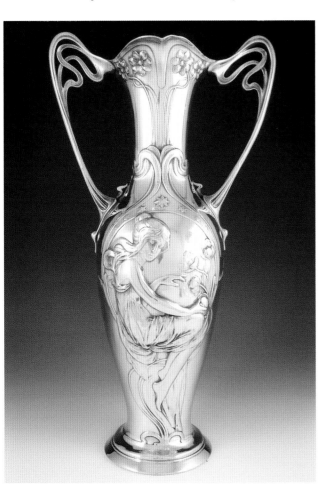

1.24 WMF Art Nouveau pair of green crystal-lined pewter flower vases (model 84) designed c.1906, h. 18cm. (Titus Omega)

1.23 WMF pewter vase with maiden motif c.1904, h. 46cm. (Titus Omega)

23

1.25 WMF Art Nouveau pewter flower vase (model 93m) designed c.1906, h. 24cm. (FCR Gallery London)

1.26 WMF Art Nouveau crystal-lined pewter flower vase (model 331a) designed c.1906, h. 36cm. (FCR Gallery London)

1.27 WMF Art Nouveau crystal-lined pewter flower vase (model 78) designed c.1906, h. 19cm. (Titus Omega)

1.28 WMF pair of Art Nouveau engraved crystal-lined pewter flower vases with musicians (models 163 and 163a) designed c.1906, h. 34.5cm. (FCR Gallery London)

1.30 WMF Secessionist crystal-lined pewter biscuit box (model 183) designed c.1906, h. 20cm. (FCR Gallery London)

1.29 WMF Art Nouveau crystal-lined pewter biscuit box (model 231) designed c.1906, h. 23cm. (Titus Omega)

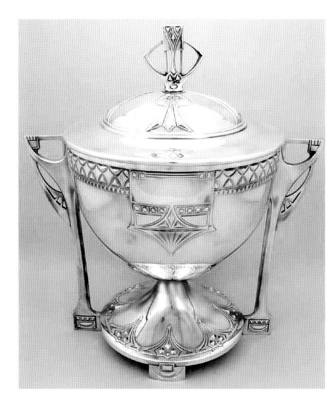

1.31 WMF Art Nouveau pewter wine cooler (model 237) designed c.1906, h. 25.5cm. (FCR Gallery London)

1.32 WMF Art Nouveau crystal-lined pewter punch bowl (model 84) designed c.1906, capacity 15 pints. (Titus Omega)

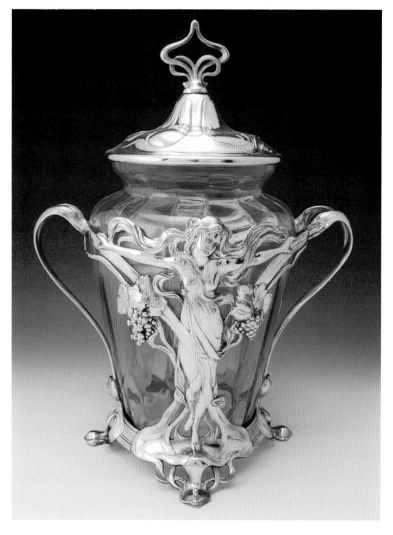

1.33 WMF rare Art Nouveau crystal-lined pewter punch bowl designed c.1907, h. 40cm. (Titus Omega)

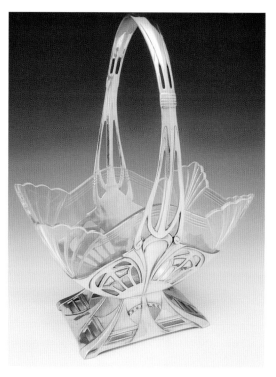

1.34 WMF Secessionist crystal-lined flower basket (model 544) designed c.1906, h. 37cm. (Titus Omega)

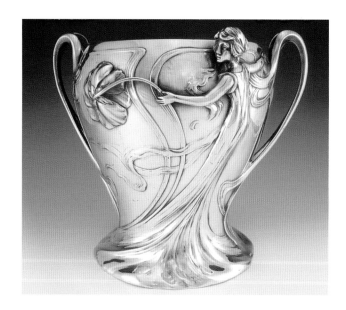

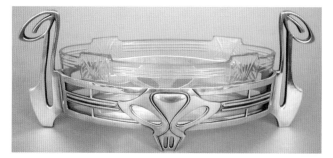

1.36 WMF Secessionist crystal-lined pewter oval flower dish (model 343) designed c.1906, w. 24.5cm. (FCR Gallery London)

1.35 WMF Art Nouveau pewter flower pot/wine cooler (model 290) designed c.1906, h. 24.5cm. (Titus Omega)

1.37 WMF Art Nouveau pewter flower dish lined with blue crystal,
designed c.1906, h. 19.5cm. (Titus Omega)

1.38 WMF Art Nouveau pewter oval flower dish (model 590) lined with
etched crystal, designed c.1906, w. 31cm. (FCR Gallery London)

1.39 WMF Art Nouveau pewter oval flower dish with butterfly motif and lined with blue crystal, designed c.1906, w. 42cm. (FCR Gallery London)

1.40 WMF Art Nouveau crystal-lined pewter oval flower dish designed c.1906, w. 48cm. (Titus Omega)

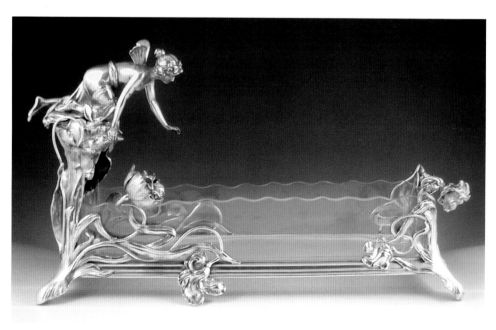

1.41 WMF Art Nouveau crystal-lined pewter oblong flower dish (model 444) designed c.1906, w. 53cm. (Titus Omega)

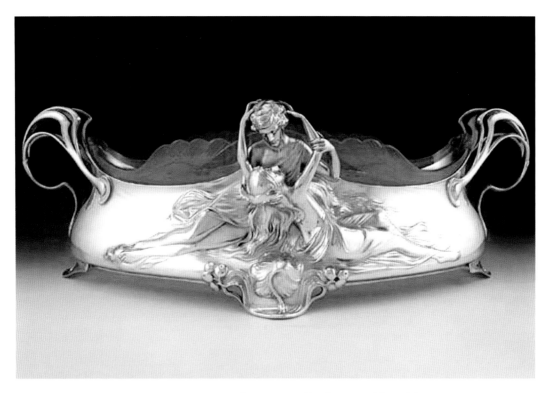

1.42 WMF Art Nouveau 'The Lovers' crystal-lined pewter oval flower dish
(model 85) designed c.1906, w. 52cm. (Titus Omega)

1.43 WMF Art Nouveau crystal-lined pewter oval flower dish (model 331)
designed c.1906 w. 49cm. (FCR Gallery London)

1.44 WMF Art Nouveau pewter visiting card tray (model 246) designed
c.1906, h. 21.5cm. (FCR Gallery London)

1.46 WMF Art Nouveau pewter double fruit or sweet dish (model 169/a)
designed c.1906, h. 23cm. (FCR Gallery London)

1.45 WMF Art Nouveau pewter visiting card tray (model 4) designed c.1906,
w. 27cm. (FCR Gallery London)

1.47 WMF Art Nouveau pewter and etched crystal inkstand with envelope carrier (model 268) designed c.1906, w. 26.5cm. (FCR Gallery London)

1.48 WMF rare Art Nouveau pewter stationery stand designed c.1908, h. 18cm. (FCR Gallery London)

1.49 WMF Art Nouveau pewter inkstand (model 168) designed c.1906, h. 19cm. (FCR Gallery London)

1.50 WMF Secessionist pewter inkwell (model 120/k) designed c.1906, w. 18cm. (FCR Gallery London)

1.51 WMF Classical pewter chamber candlestick (model 69) designed c.1906, w. 17cm. (FCR Gallery London)

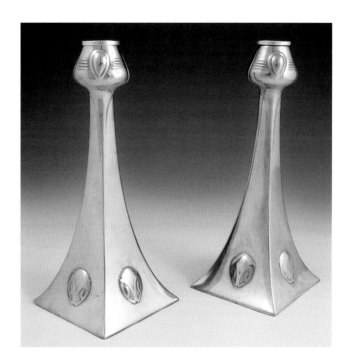

1.52 WMF Secessionist pewter candlesticks (model 120a) designed c.1906, h. 17cm. (FCR Gallery London)

1.53 WMF Secessionist pewter candlesticks (model 132a) designed by Albin Müller c.1906, h. 23.5cm. (Titus Omega)

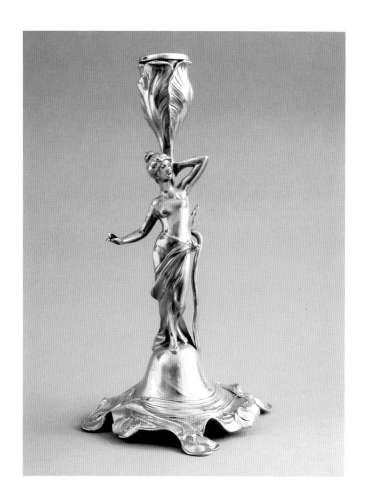

1.54 WMF Art Nouveau pewter 'Adam' candlestick (model 167) designed c.1906, h. 19.5cm. (FCR Gallery London)

1.55 WMF Art Nouveau pewter 'Eve' candlestick (model 167a) designed c.1906, h. 19.5cm. (FCR Gallery London)

1.56 WMF Art Nouveau pewter twin branch maiden candelabra (model 269/2) designed c.1906, h. 26.5cm. (FCR Gallery London)

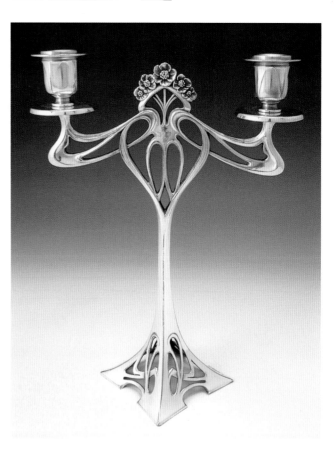

1.57 WMF pair of Art Nouveau pewter maiden candelabrum (model 16/4 169/a4) designed c.1906, h. 49.5cm. (Titus Omega)

1.58 WMF Secessionist 'Eiffel Tower' pewter candelabra (model 192/2) designed c.1906, h. 32cm. (Titus Omega)

1.59 WMF pair of Art Nouveau 'Eiffel Tower' pewter candlesticks (model 92) designed c.1906, h. 28.5cm. (FCR Gallery London)

1.60 WMF Art Nouveau pewter and brass clock c.1906, h. 41cm. (Titus Omega)

1.61 WMF Art Nouveau pewter visiting card tray (model 290) designed c.1906, d. 28.5cm. (FCR Gallery London)

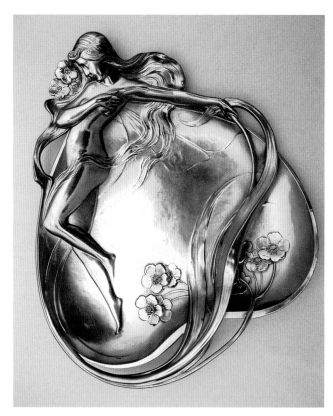

1.62 WMF Art Nouveau pewter visiting card tray (model 232) designed c.1906, w. 27.5cm. (FCR Gallery London)

1.63 WMF Art Nouveau pewter visiting card tray (model 249) designed c.1906, w. 26cm. (FCR Gallery London)

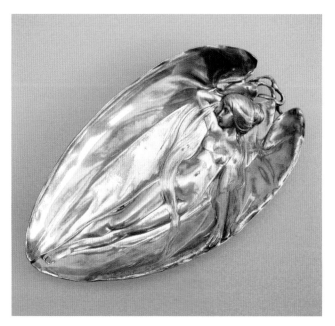

1.64 WMF Art Nouveau pewter jewel tray (model 213) designed c.1906, w. 15cm. (FCR Gallery London)

1.65 WMF Art Nouveau pewter toilet table tray (model 229) designed c.1906, w. 25.5cm. (FCR Gallery London)

1.66 WMF pewter visiting card tray (model 245) c.1906, l. 27cm.
(Titus Omega)

1.67 WMF Art Nouveau pewter jewel tray (model 211) designed c.1906, w. 23cm. (FCR Gallery London)

1.68 WMF rare Art Nouveau pewter jewel tray designed c.1906, w. 18.5cm. (FCR Gallery London)

1.69 WMF Art Nouveau pewter visiting card tray humorously modelled as a frog playing a flute. Designed c.1908, w. 23.5cm. (FCR Gallery London)

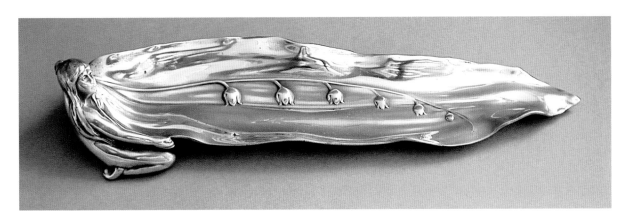

1.70 WMF Art Nouveau pewter hatpin tray (model 215) designed c.1906,
w. 23cm. (FCR Gallery London)

1.71 WMF Secessionist pewter visiting card tray (model 120)
designed c.1906, w. 25.5cm. (FCR Gallery London)

1.72 WMF Art Nouveau pewter visiting card tray (model 369)
designed c.1906, h. 25.5cm. (FCR Gallery London)

1.73 WMF Art Nouveau pewter lamp (model 169a) designed c.1906, h. 59cm. This lamp would have originally had a silk shade. (FCR Gallery London)

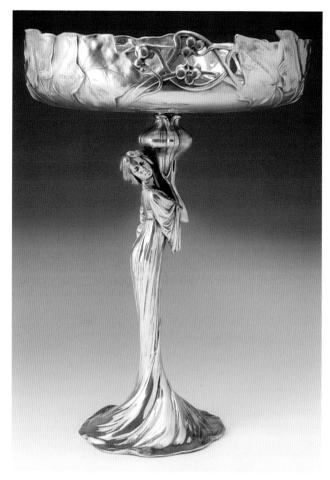

1.74 WMF Art Nouveau pewter tazza (model 469a) designed c.1906, h. 41cm. (Titus Omega)

1.75 WMF Art Nouveau pewter tazza (model 427) designed c.1906, h. 36cm. (FCR Gallery London)

1.76 WMF Art Nouveau pewter coffee set (model 293) designed c.1906, coffee pot ⅔ pint. (FCR Gallery London)

1.77 WMF Art Nouveau pewter cigarette box (model 229k) designed c.1906, 14.5cm. (FCR Gallery London)

1.78 WMF Secessionist pewter bell (model 48) designed c.1906, h. 15cm. (Didier Antiques)

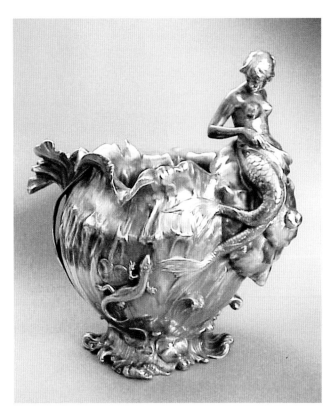

1.79 WMF Art Nouveau pewter wine cooler (model 112) c.1906, h. 25cm.
(FCR Gallery London)

1.80 WMF Art Nouveau pewter jewel box (model 90) c.1906, w. 15cm.
(FCR Gallery London)

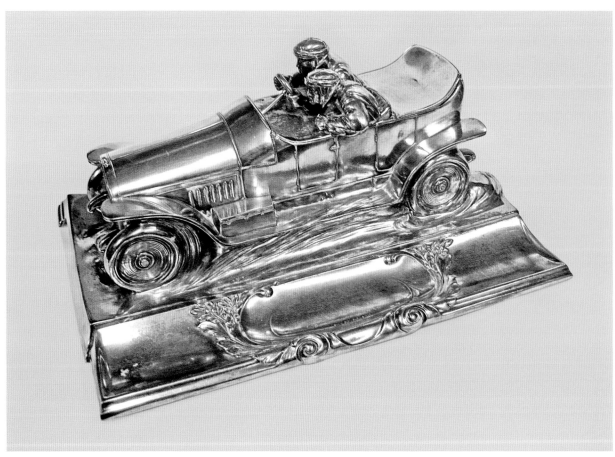

1.81 WMF Art Nouveau racing car inkstand c.1909, w. 31cm.
(Photo: Sjöström Antiques Stockholm)

1.82 WMF pewter and crystal neo classical vase (model 304a) c.1906, h. 34cm. (FCR Gallery London)

1.83 WMF pewter mounted green glass decanter (model 191) 1906, 1.5 pints, h. 36.5cm. (FCR Gallery London)

Examples of WMF Marks

J.P. Kayser Sohn (Kayserzinn)
1885 – 1930

Kayserzinn produced some of the most extraordinary pewter of the Art Nouveau period. The forms were heavy but never clumsy, like molten lava encrusted with fossilised insects, animals and plant life. This seminal German firm was paramount in popularising pewter as a modern 20th century medium.

J.P. Kayser Sohn, the company producing Kayserzinnwaren (Kayser pewter ware) was a family run business founded in 1885 by Jean P. Kayser in Krefeld-Bochum near Dusseldorf. They made a wide range of traditional designs in pewter, many with hunting motifs. The reputation of the company was further enhanced by the introduction of a leadless pewter alloy which was suitable for table items. Jean's son Englebert helped to develop this improved alloy and he is also credited with introducing one of the first modern beer tankards to Germany. These domestic items proved to be highly popular, contributing significantly to the success of the company, and in 1894 a design studio was set up in Cologne. Here they set out producing pewter items with an artistic integrity sympathetic to the Arts and Crafts movement.

The designer Hugo Leven (1874-1956) joined the firm around 1895. He helped modernise their pewter range with a fresh Jugendstil (youth style) approach to design. Other artists employed were Karl Geyer (a noted architect), Hermann Fauser, Karl Berghof and Professor Johann Christian Kroner, a popular painter of hunting scenes.[1]

Leven's designs were conceptually organic, deriving much of their inspiration from nature. His abstract constructions incorporated realistically fashioned details of plants and wildlife, whilst retaining a degree of charm and humour. This is evident in his use of animals such as a stylised auk alca-torda (a bird similar to a penguin) to create the body of a wine jug (Plate 1.89) and a smiling bat in his design for a candelabra (Plate 1.85). These unusual pewter items were shaped in clay first and then cast iron moulds were produced using the models. The clay appears to have been naïvely impressed with finger marks in a free and childlike manner. If you visualise these pieces in their original clay form you can begin to understand the sublime nature of Leven's persona as a sculptor. The very essence of his shapes transform well to the pewter medium with reflected light filling the crevices like tidal rock pools (Plate 1.95).

By the start of the 20th century the Kayserzinn factory was producing hundreds of designs, many of which were in the Art Nouveau style. They won gold medals at important exhibitions in Paris (1900), Turin (1902) and St Louis (1904). Production was at its height around 1902 and the firm expanded to employ hundreds of workers. At this point in time Kayserzinn had become one of the largest importers of tin in the world, giving an insight into just how much the firm had grown.[2]

Having a good distribution system was an important factor in Kayserzinn's success, but it was also a matter of having the right product at the right time. This was an exciting and transitional period for design in Germany. The Darmstadt Art Colony was the centre for the country's vernacular Arts and Crafts movement; it was a hotbed for international design and had a profound effect on the tastes of a nation which was now at the forefront of the avant garde movement. Kayserzinn was also one of the first modern manufacturers to market pewter through the use of a lavishly illustrated catalogue. This means of mass exposure allowed the firm to achieve world wide recognition and popularity.

Arthur Lasenby Liberty, the founder of the well known London emporium, was quick to recognise the commercial potential of Kayserzinn pewter. He began importing it around 1895 and it was subsequently an enormous success. The popularity of Kayserzinn also impelled Liberty to seek out other German pewter lines and it is likely that its success at Liberty & Co was the inspiration behind the Tudric range of pewter which heralded the revival of artistic pewter in Great Britain.[3]

1. See *Kayserzinn Musterbuch 1907*, (Introduction by Gerhard P. Woeckel), Verlag Dry, Munchen, 1982.

2. See Note 1.
3. Tilbrook, Adrian J., *The Designs of Archibald Knox*, Ornament Press, 1976.

1.84 Kayserzinn pewter rose bowl (model 4514) c.1906, w. 22cm.
(FCR Gallery London)

Despite their initial success, by 1910 Kayserzinn's popularity was on a downward turn. The demand for artistic pewter was replaced with other metals and styles and even large companies like WMF were gearing their production towards *faux repoussé* copper and brass. By the First World War, Kayserzinn were reduced to a skeleton staff, employing only a handful of workers. The company continued to produce many of their old designs and had little success with pieces in the Art Deco style. In 1930 the company filed for bankruptcy.

Kayserzinn pewter was sold with the option of three finishes: highly polished silver, gold gilt, or bronze patinated. The silver finish proved the most popular and the majority of pieces available to the collector today have remnants of these finishes.

The company had a distinctive way of signing their wares and most pieces are clearly marked utilising either a round or an oval lozenge. Many pieces are marked with a number between 4000-4889, but individual artists/designers did not sign their pieces with a monogram and only the trademark name of Kayserzinn appears alongside the production number.

Kayserzinn oxidises to a dark matte pewter finish with age. Much of the surface decoration is executed in low relief which can cause problems with design loss if over polished. There is also the problem of flaking which leads to pitting in severe cases. This surface deterioration is only prevented by stripping the pewter back to the base metal and then carefully cutting back (avoiding any loss of design) to the delicate relief, before re-polishing the piece by hand.

1.85 Kayserzinn pewter bat candelabrum (model 4506) designed by
Hugo Leven, h. 32cm. (FCR Gallery London)

1.86 Kayserzinn pewter covered tureen (model 4504) designed by Hugo Leven
c.1906, h. 17cm. (Titus Omega)

1.87 Kayserzinn pewter pair of five-branch candelabrum (model 4486)
designed by Hugo Leven c.1906, h. 48cm. (Titus Omega)

1.88 Kayserzinn pewter pair of candlesticks (model 4521) designed by Hugo Leven c.1906, h. 30cm. (FCR Gallery London)

1.89 Kayserzinn pewter jug depicting an auk (model 4433) designed by Hugo Leven c.1906, h. 29cm. (FCR Gallery London)

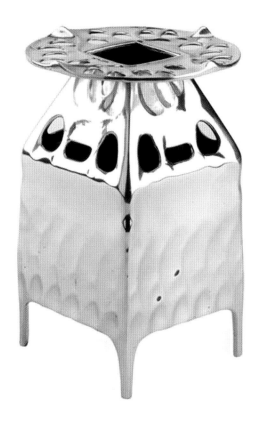

1.90 Kayserzinn pewter flower vase (model 4541) by Karl Berghof c.1904, h. 18.5cm. (Photo: Lyon & Turnbull)

1.91 Kayserzinn pewter liqueur service depicting an auk (model 4358) designed by Hugo Leven c.1906, w. 34cm. (FCR Gallery London)

1.92 Kayserzinn pewter covered tureen (model 4556) designed by Hugo Leven c.1906, w. 21cm. (FCR Gallery London)

1.93 Kayserzinn pewter jardinière with squirrel motif (model 4430) designed by Hugo Leven c.1906, w. 19cm. (FCR Gallery London)

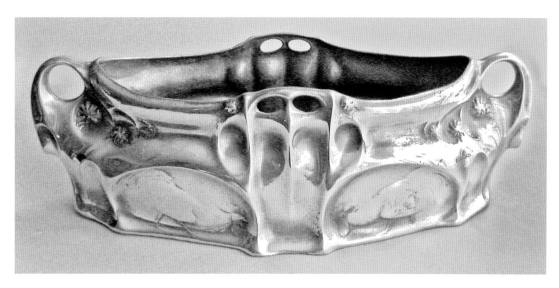

1.94 Kayserzinn pewter jardinière (model 4511) designed by Hugo Leven c.1906, w. 22cm. (FCR Gallery London)

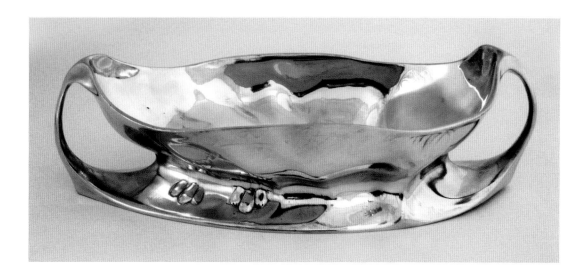

1.95 Kayserzinn pewter jardinière model 4461 designed by Hugo Leven c.1906 w. 34cm. (FCR Gallery London)

1.96 Kayserzinn pewter watering can with snail motif (model 4205) designed by Hugo Leven c.1905, h. 21.5cm. (Titus Omega)

1.97 Kayserzinn pewter photo frame (model 4222) designed c.1906, h. 28cm. (Photo: Titus Omega)

1.98 Kayserzinn pewter meat cover (model 4563), w. 32cm. (FCR Gallery London)

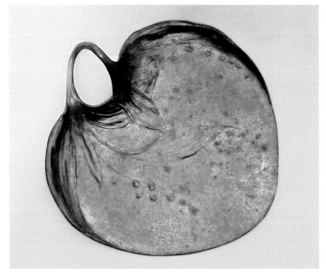

1.99 Kayserzinn pewter tray depicting a lily pad (model 4597) c.1905, d. 20cm. (FCR Gallery London)

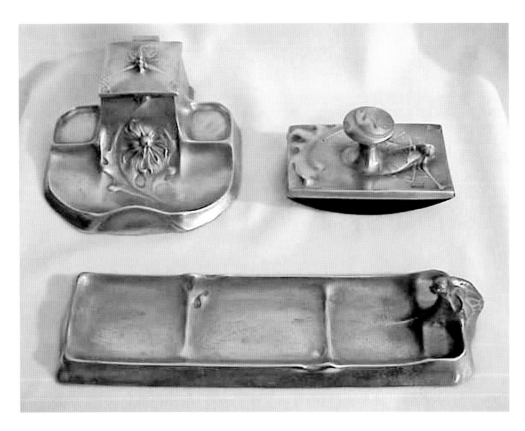

1.100 Kayserzinn pewter desk set including ink, blotter and pen tray (models 4680, 4685, 4681) designed by Hugo Leven c.1906, ink 15 x 15cm, pen tray w. 33cm, blotter w. 14cm. (FCR Gallery London)

1.101 Kayserzinn pewter breakfast set (model 4473) c.1906, eggcup:
h. 10cm. (Photo: Jacksons, Stockholm)

1.102 Kayserzinn pewter 3 piece tea set (model 4510) designed by
Hugo Leven c.1902, teapot: h. 16.5cm. (Didier Antiques)

1.103 Kayserzinn pewter 3 piece tea set (model 4402) on tray (model 4401) designed by Hugo Leven c.1902, teapot: h. 16.0cm. (FCR Gallery London)

1.104 Kayserzinn pewter cigar lighter depicting a steamboat (model 4428) c.1906, w. 20cm. (Martyn Stamp)

1.105 Kayserzinn pewter cachepot (model 4596) c.1906, h. 9.5cm.
(FCR Gallery London)

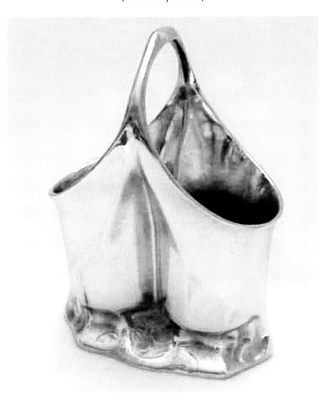

1.106 Kayserzinn pewter vase with floral motif (model 4312)
1908, h. 31cm. (FCR Gallery London)

1.107 Kayserzinn pewter cigarette basket (model 4535)
designed by Hugo Leven c.1905, h. 14cm. (FCR Gallery London)

Examples of Kayserzinn Marks

Orivit Metallwarenfabrik
1894 – 1905

Orivit Metallwarenfabrik was founded in 1894 by Wilhelm Ferdinand Hubert Schmitz (1863-1939) in Bedburg, just outside Cologne. The company quickly acquired a favourable reputation for their production of quality silver, brass, bronze and silver-electroplated domestic metalware.

In 1897 Orivit began to produce a range of pewterware called Schmitz-Edelzinn. The formula[1] was one of the first modern adaptations of this traditional material and was soon incorporated into the company's innovative production output. Many items made by Orivit were silver-plated or gilded and then finished with an antique patination which added a rich and luxurious finish to the base metal. The company is also noted for combining pewter mounts with ceramic and glass vases and bowls. This created a stunning effect by contrasting the sinuous silvery metal with colourful faience and etched and enamelled glass. It is not known which firm provided the Keramik vessels, although it is thought that much of the glass was produced by the Belgian firm Val St. Lambert (Plates 1.121, 1.122, 1.123 and 1.127).

The company had a number of first-rate designers who either worked in house or were paid for individual designs. These artists included Walter Scherf (who went on to found the Osiris firm), Hermann Gradl and Georges Charles Couldray (a noted French figurative sculptor). Stylistically, Orivit covered a wide range of commercial designs; traditional items with Neo-Classical motifs (Plate 1.133) were contrasted with the more experimental Art Nouveau floral and naturalistic forms. These were quite often sculpted in low relief decoration, adorning trays, bowls and vases (Plates 1.126, 1.129 and 1.130). The use of three dimensional figures, some designed by Georges Charles Coudray, were also extremely successful (Plate 1.108 is in the style of Coudray but there are no clear attributions).

Orivit won a gold medal at the Paris Exposition Universelle in 1900 and this prompted the production of their first printed catalogue. The company then expanded greatly, opening showrooms on the Avenue de L'Opera in Paris and also in the thriving artistic centre of Vienna. However, this growth proved disastrous and the company fell into financial difficulties around 1905. There are no surviving records as to exactly why Orivit collapsed, but their saviour turned out to be their greatest rival, the massive multinational company Württembergische Metallwarenfabrik. Through buying Orivit, WMF acquired their innovative technology, in particular the Huber-Presverfahren – an enormous pressure driven sheet metal press, capable of previously unattainable mass production techniques.[2] WMF continued the manufacture of many Orivit designs up until the First World War.

---

1. Approximately 89% tin, 8 % antimony, 2 % copper and 1% silver.

2. *Orivit Zinn des Jugendstils aus Koln*, Elisabeth Ch Vaupel, Kölnisches Stadt Museum, 1991.

1.108 Orivit pewter Art Nouveau four-branch candelabrum (model 2211) c.1904, h. 31cm. (Titus Omega)

1.109 Orivit figural pewter lamp (model 3855) 1904, h. 53cm. (Collection Sergei Glebov)

1.110 Orivit bronze patinated pewter clock with enamelled dial (model 2432) 1904, h. 34.8cm. It has been suggested that this clock was designed by Peter Behrens, however no documentary proof exists and it is more likely to be a Walter Scherf design. (Quinty's Art Nouveau)

1.111 Orivit pewter desk lamp in the Art Nouveau style (model 2387) c.1905, h. 37cm. (Doré antiques)

1.112 Orivit pewter Art Nouveau candlesticks (model 2284) c.1904, h. 17.6cm. (FCR Gallery, London)

1.113 Orivit pewter and ceramic jardinière (model 2576) c.1904, h. 25.5cm. (Titus Omega)

1.114 Orivit gilt pewter mounted ceramic vase
(model 2560) c.1906, h. 13cm.
(Quinty's Art Nouveau)

1.115 Orivit pewter and copper enamel jardinière
(model 2576) c.1904,
h. 25.5cm. (Titus Omega)

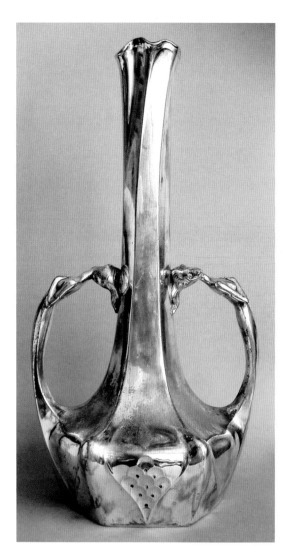

1.116 Orivit pewter Art Nouveau vase (model 1188) c.1904,
h. 38.5cm. (Robert Petersen, Melborne)

1.117 Orivit pewter and ceramic Art Nouveau vase (model
2502) c.1900, h. 27.5cm. (Titus Omega)

1.118 Orivit pewter and ceramic Art Nouveau vase (model 2537) c.1904, h. 24 cm. (Titus Omega)

1.120 Orivit pewter and glass Art Nouveau vase (model 2547) c.1904, h. 30.2cm. (Titus Omega)

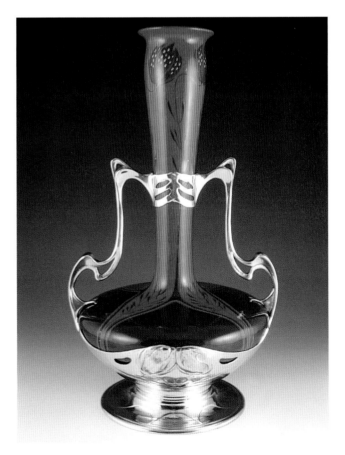

1.119 Orivit pewter and ceramic Art Nouveau vase (model 2502) c.1904, h 27.5cm. (Titus Omega)

1.122 Orivit pewter and glass Art Nouveau vase (model 2561) c.1904,
h. 20.5cm (FCR Gallery London)

(Left) **1.121** Orivit pewter and glass Art Nouveau vase (model 2545) c.1904,
h. 42.2 cm. The glass was most likely made by Val St. Lambert.
(Titus Omega)

1.123 Orivit pewter and glass Aesthetic movement vase (model 5031) c.1904, h. 36cm. (FCR Gallery London)

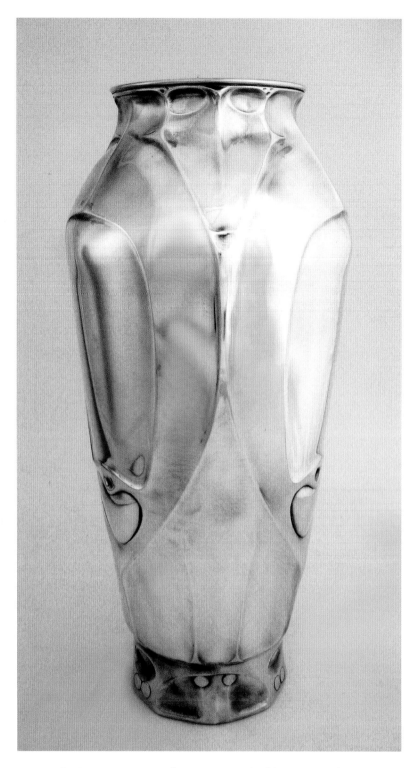

1.124 Orivit pewter monumental Art Nouveau vase (model 5031) c.1905, h. 61cm. (FCR Gallery London)

1.125 Orivit pewter and cut crystal Art Nouveau Liqueur set (models 2192, 2193, 2194) c.1904, tray: h. 22.5cm, w. 40.7cm. (FCR Gallery London)

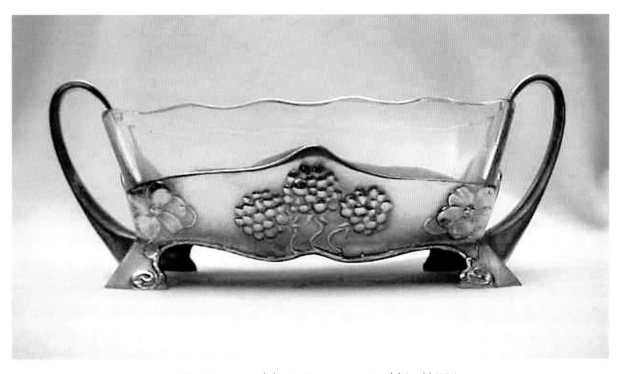

1.126 Orivit pewter and glass Art Nouveau compotiere dish (model 2106) c.1904, w. 28cm. (FCR Gallery London)

1.127 Orivit pewter and glass Art Nouveau tazza (model 2582) c.1904, w. 25.2cm. The etched and enamelled glass is most likely by Val St. Lambert. (FCR Gallery London)

1.128 Orivit gilt pewter and glass Art Nouveau champagne coupe (model 2549) c.1904, h. 12.9cm. (Titus Omega)

1.129 Orivit pewter Art Nouveau wall plaque (model 2338) designed by sculptor Hermann Gradl c.1904, d. 51cm. (Valmar Antiques)

1.130 Orivit pewter Art Nouveau tray with mistletoe motif (model 2025) designed by Hermann Gradl c.1904, d. 25cm. (FCR Gallery London)

1.131 Orivit pewter Secessionist cedar lined cigarette box (model 3896) c.1911, w. 16.3cm. (FCR Gallery London)

1.132 Orivit pewter and ebony Art Nouveau jug (model 2615) c.1904, h. 28cm. (FCR Gallery London)

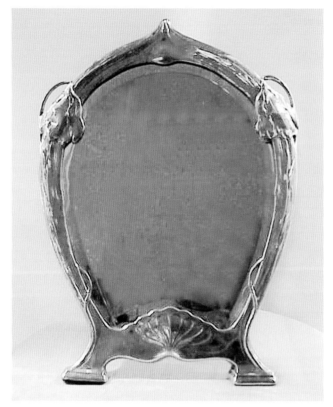

1.134 Orivit pewter Art Nouveau toilet mirror (model 2117) c.1904, h. 31cm. (FCR Gallery London)

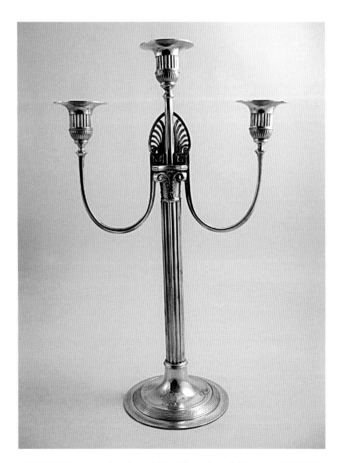

1.133 Orivit pewter three-branch Neo Classical candelabrum (model 3505) c.1906, h. 44.5cm. (FCR Gallery London)

1.135 Orivit pewter Art Nouveau toilet mirror (model 2280) c.1904,
h. 37.6cm. (Titus Omega)

Examples of Orivit Marks

1.136 Osiris gilt pewter mounted ceramic vase (model 992) designed by
Friedrich Adler c.1905, h. 23cm and d. 25cm. The ceramic bowl is by Zsolnay,
the pewter is marked 'Osiris'. (Collection Sergei Glebov)

Walter Scherf & Co. (Osiris, Isis Pewter)
1899 – 1914

Walter Scherf & Co. was perhaps the most inspired of the German pewter design companies and was founded as Metallwarenfabrik fur Kleinkunst Walter Scherf & Co. in 1899. Scherf had worked for Orivit in Cologne and was well versed in modern production and marketing techniques.

Scherf studied with Richard Riemerschmid and Paul Haustien at the Bavarian Museum of Handicrafts, Nuremberg. These men were respected designers in their own right and were highly regarded at the time as successful teachers. Their guidance had a profound influence on Scherf and he designed many of the innovative Osiris models himself, incorporating his inspired understanding of naturalistic form. Many of the pieces integrated birds, animals and organic plant forms as part of their structure (Plates 1.141, 1.144 and 1.158).

In addition, Scherf was experienced in his trade and understood his market. He had the foresight to commission work from some of the leading designers of the period, including Friedrich Adler (Plates 1.136, 1.137, 1.138, 1.139, 1.141, 1.143, 1.144, 1.145, 1.156, 1.163 and 1.166), Joseph Maria Olbrich and Peter Behrens.[1] Osiris won a number of accolades at international exhibitions including a Certificate of Honour at the 1902 Turin Exhibition and both first and second prize at the 1904 St. Louis World Exhibition.

In 1902 Scherf brought out a new line of pewter called Isis and this then replaced the previous name Osiris. The Isis mark was stamped along side the Osiris mark and although the pewter formula remained the same, many items were gilded or lavishly electroplated with silver. Some items were also marked with the master class mark of the Bayerisches Gewerbemuseum (The Nuremberg Handicrafts Guild, see page 83).

Art Nouveau, like many radical styles that define the spirit of the times, went out of fashion. It was as if the world were eagerly awaiting the next wave or trend. The first ten years of the new century were a time of opulent excesses, but then the European economic downturn played a role in the demise of the lucrative pewter market. The smaller factories and workshops either faced bankruptcy and closure, or were absorbed by larger predatory companies.

In 1906 Scherf changed the name of the company to Isis Werke Gmbh Kunstgewerblicher Erzeugnisse (Commercial Art Products)[2] and they continued to produce a large number of models which were sumptuously decorated and uneconomical. The company rapidly began sinking into debt, and by 1909, it was on the verge of closure. This catastrophic crisis led to Scherf's dismissal from the company and he died days later; he was a broken man and probably took his own life. The company survived for the next few years with a pared down range of models, but closed in 1914, just as the First World War was declared.

---

1. Behrens remains unconfirmed as a Scherf & Co. designer, however stylistically a number of Osiris models echo his work and this has led to attributions by experts (see Plates 1.150, 1.152, 1.155, 1.161, and 1.164).

2. *Modern Art of Metalware*, Brohan Museum V1, 2001 (catalogue).

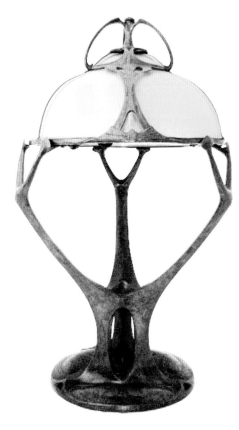

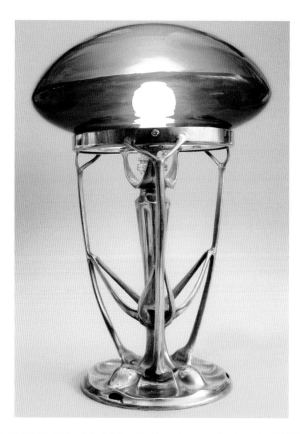

1.137 Osiris Walter Scherf & Co. 'Tischlampe' pewter glass lamp designed by Friedrich Adler 1901-1902, h. 48cm. (Quinty's)

1.138 Osiris Walter Scherf & Co. 'Tischlampe' pewter glass lamp (model 751) designed by Friedrich Adler 1901-1902, h. 41.9cm.
(FCR Gallery London)

1.139 Osiris Walter Scherf & Co. 'Tischlampe' pewter lamp with silk shade option designed by Friedrich Adler 1901-1902, h. 52cm. (Quinty's)

1.140 Osiris Walter Scherf & Co. 'Tischlampe' pewter glass lamp with bat motif (model 751) designed by Walter Scherf 1901-1902, h. 41.9cm. (Quinty's)

1.141 Osiris Walter Scherf & Co. 'Lampe' pewter lamp (model 750) designed
by Friedrich Adler with a Loetz glass shade 1901-1902, h. 38cm.
(Titus Omega)

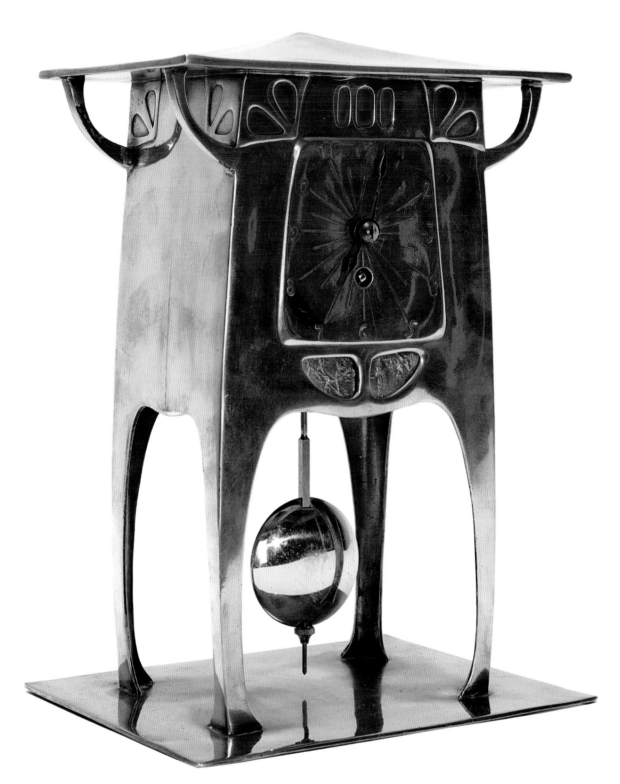

1.142 Osiris pewter and enamel clock. Although it is unsigned, this clock is
stylistically similar to many other Osiris pieces. It was most likely designed by
Walter Scherf c.1905, h. 19cm. (Collection Sergei Glebov)

1.143 Osiris pewter clock with gilt dial (model 762) designed by Friedrich Adler c.1901, h. 23cm. (Quinty's)

1.144 Osiris pewter clock with gilt dial (model 761) designed by Friedrich Adler c.1901, h. 36cm. (Quinty's)

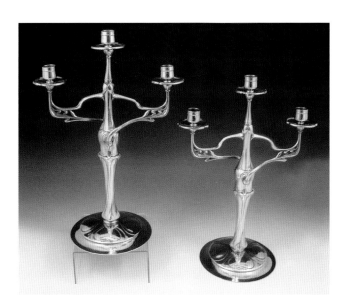

1.145 Osiris Walter Scherf & Co. pewter candelabra (model 600) designed by Friedrich Adler 1900, h. 41cm. This was also made in two, four and five-branch models. (Titus Omega)

1.146 Osiris Walter Scherf & Co. pewter candelabrum designed by Walter Scherf 1900 h. 34.5cm. (FCR Gallery London)

1.147 Osiris pewter champagne bucket or flower, cache pot with green cabochons (model 960) 1902-3, h. 26cm. (Collection Sergei Glebov)

1.148 Osiris gilt pewter mounted glass vase designed by Walter Scherf c.1901, h. 23cm. (Quinty's)

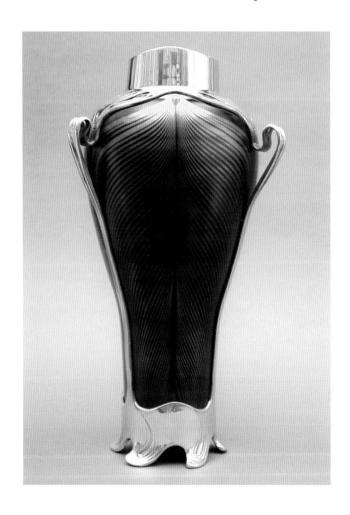

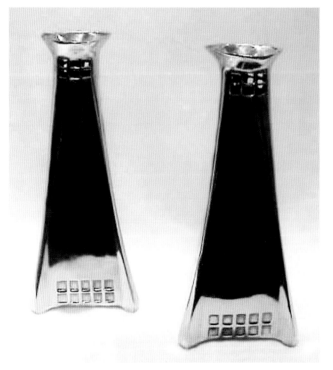

1.150 Osiris A pair of pewter spill vases in the style of Peter Behrens c.1905, h. 15cm. (FCR Gallery London)

1.149 Osiris Walter Scherf & Co. pewter mounted Loetz phanomen glass vase (model 1902) designed by Walter Scherf, h. 24.4cm. (FCR Gallery London)

1.152 Osiris a pewter crystal lined punch bowl design attributed to Peter Behrens c.1905, d. 30cm. (Titus Omega)

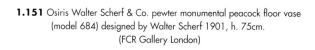

1.151 Osiris Walter Scherf & Co. pewter monumental peacock floor vase (model 684) designed by Walter Scherf 1901, h. 75cm.
(FCR Gallery London)

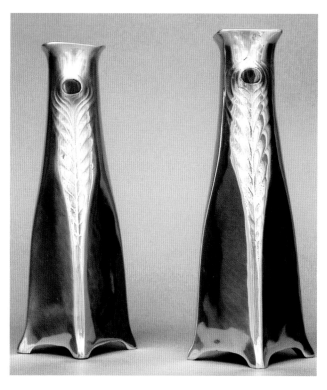

1.154 Osiris Walter Scherf & Co. pewter and enamel spill vases by Walter Scherf 1904, h. 18cm. (Titus Omega)

1.153 Osiris Walter Scherf & Co. pewter and glass vase designed by Walter Scherf 1901, h. 41. (FCR Gallery London)

1.155 Osiris pewter and glass rosebowl design attributed to Peter Behrens c.1905, w. 35cm. (Collection Sergei Glebov)

1.156 (below, left) Osiris Walter Scherf & Co. pewter and glass tazza designed by Friedrich Adler model 587 h. 16.0cm. (FCR Gallery London)

1.157 (below, right) Osiris Walter Scherf & Co. pewter and glass water jug c.1903, h. 16cm. (FCR Gallery London)

1.158 (below, centre) Osiris Walter Scherf & Co. pewter and purple glass oval flower dish designed by Walter Scherf c.1904-1905, w. 27.5cm. (Titus Omega)

1.159 Pewter mounted glass Art Nouveau punch bowl set with 6 stemmed glasses c.1905, height of glasses: 12cm. (Titus Omega)

1.160 Osiris Walter Scherf & Co. pewter and enamel tea caddy/tobacco jar, designer unknown, but similar to a design in silver by Archibald Knox c.1905, h. 20.5cm. (FCR Gallery London)

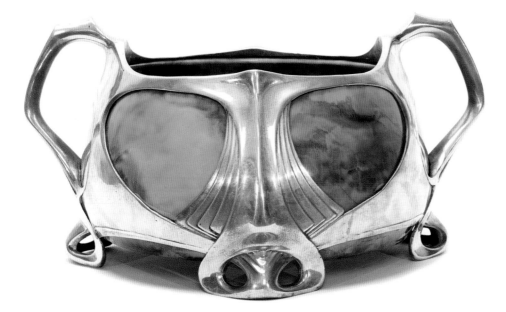

1.161 Osiris pewter mounted ceramic rose bowl (model 791) in the style of Peter Behrens c.1905, marked 'Osiris', w. 43cm. (Collection Sergei Glebov)

1.162 Osiris pewter rose bowl inset with turquoise cabochons c.1905, unmarked, d 30cm. This bowl is in the style of Archibald Knox and is similar to another Knox inspired design shown in plate 1.160. (Collection Sergei Glebov)

1.163 Osiris Walter Scherf & Co. pewter cedar lined cigarette box (model 679) designed by Friedrich Adler c.1903, w. 13.5cm. (FCR Gallery London)

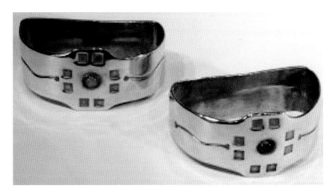

1.164 Osiris Walter Scherf & Co. pewter napkin rings inlaid with abalone possibly designed by Peter Behrens c.1904, w. 8cm. (FCR Gallery London)

1.165 Osiris Walter Scherf & Co. pewter with green glass cabochons photo frame c.1902, h. 13.5cm This appears in the 1909 Liberty Yuletide catalogue under 'Pewter in quaint and useful shapes'. (FCR Gallery London)

1.166 Osiris Perter and crystal cigarette box designed by Friedrich Adler c.1903, h. 15cm. (Quinty's Art Nouveau)

1.167 Osiris pewter charger probably designed by Friedrich Adler c.1905, d. 35cm. (CARNAVALET, Köln)

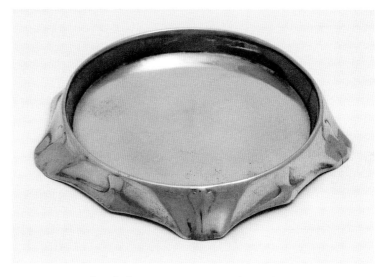

1.168 Osiris Walter Scherf & Co. pewter wine coaster designed by Walter Scherf 1900, d. 10cm. (FCR Gallery London)

Examples of Osiris Marks

The example on the right shows both the Osiris mark and that of the Nuremberg Handicrafts Guild.

Orion Pewter
1903 – 1905

Orion was founded by Georg Friedrich Schmitt (1859-1938) and first started producing artistic pewter in 1903. The Nuremberg factory manufactured some interesting designs, but the items lacked the spirited originality of those from other firms, notably the Osiris range. Orion produced a catalogue illustrating over 200 models covering a range of products from tableware to cabinet pieces.[1]

Schmitt was a thorn in Walter Scherf's side from the outset, however. He was a factory owner, not a designer, and his business acumen made it possible to succeed where Scherf had failed by profitably marketing a similar range of pewterware. The company made up for the lack of artistic direction by commissioning Friedrich Adler, one of Osiris's most notable designers, to produce a number of pieces (Plates 1.170, 1.171, 1.173, 1.174, 1.175, 1.176, 1.178, 1.182 and 1.184). Again, this must have been a huge blow to Scherf's ego as his company had previously been Nuremberg's market leader. It is also thought, based on stylistic comparison, that Peter Behrens designed a number of Orion pieces. This is unrecorded and speculative, but as Behrens is known to have submitted designs to WMF, it is not unrealistic to conclude that some designs were purchased by other companies as well.

Orion pewter was well crafted and a number of finishes were possible such as silver, copper plating and gilding. The company also used cabochons in green glass to accent the polished surfaces. Orion emulated Osiris by producing a number of pewter mounts for glass and ceramics. The vase designed by Adler (Plate 1.170) is exquisitely crafted and although many were produced in both green Loetz glass and in a more exotic speckled amber, the vase takes on the appearance of a one-off handcrafted original.

A number of questions have been raised over the years which challenge the integrity of the Orion firm. It is not known whether there was a link to the demise and bankruptcy of Osiris (founded by Scherf in 1900 after his

1.169 Photo of Georg Friedrich Schmitt, Nuremberg, 1895. (GDFL)

departure from Orivit) as a direct result of the formation and aggressive marketing skills of Orion. Schmitt's company all but plagiarised the Osiris house style, manufacturing a parallel range of products in an extremely limited competitive market. Orion also poached Friedrich Adler, Osiris's leading designer, and within a year of starting the company, Schmitt sold Orion to Orivit/WMF. This was a shrewd move; Schmitt was a businessman and now had the backing of a multinational company with a huge distribution network. Osiris did not fare so well, however, and Walter Scherf was dismissed in 1909.[2] WMF/Orivit continued to use a number of the designs from the Orion range of pewter until 1914.

1. *Modern Art of Metalwork*, Brohan Museum, 2001.
2. Ibid.

1.171 A gilt pewter mounted Loetz vase designed by Friedrich Adler c.1904-5, h. 15.5cm. (FCR Gallery London)

1.170 Orion pewter mounted loetz vase (model 315) designed by Friedrich Adler c.1904-5, h. 17.5cm. The pewter is finished in silver plate or gilt. The glass was either in green or amber with spots and was most likely produced at the Loetz factory. (Titus Omega)

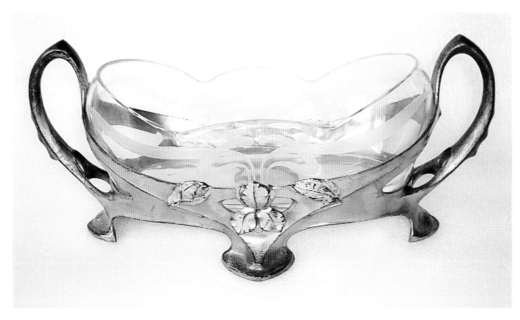

1.172 Orion gilt pewter silver leaf and etched crystal table centrepiece 1904-5, w. 26cm. (Quintys)

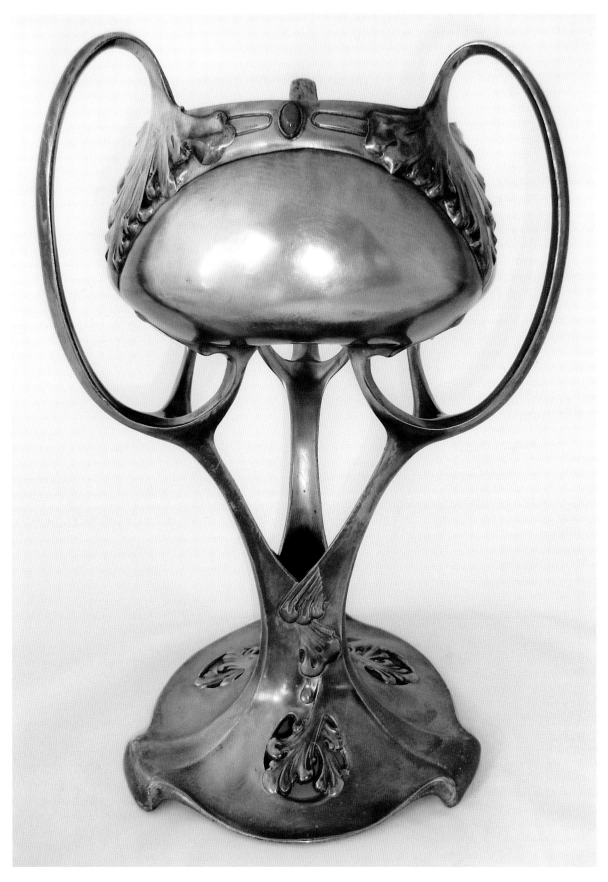

1.173 Orion gilt pewter flower vase with glass cabochons 1904-1905,
h. 40cm. (Quintys)

1.174 Orion pewter mounted biscuit box designed by Friedrich Adler
c.1904-5, h. 23cm. The pewter gilt finished with green cabochons. (Quintys)

1.175 Orion pewter tazza (model 104) designed by Friedrich Adler c.1904-5,
h. 22cm. The pewter is finished in silver plate. (FCR Gallery London)

1.176 Orion pewter tazza model with basket handles (model 104) designed by Friedrich Adler c.1904-1905, h. 22cm. The pewter finished in silver plate. (FCR Gallery London)

1.177 Orion pewter spill vases (model 315), design attributed to Peter Behrens c.1904-5, h. 15cm. The pewter finished in silver plate. (FCR Gallery London)

1.178 Orion pewter gravy boat (model 226) designed by Friedrich Adler c.1904, w. 20.5cm. (CARNAVALET, Köln)

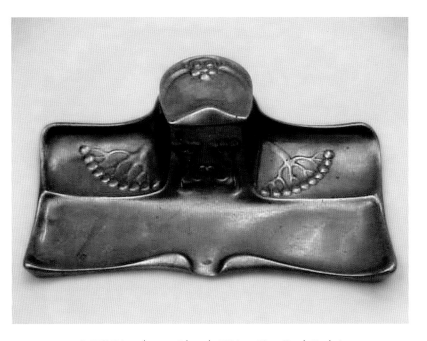

1.179 Orion gilt pewter inkstand c.1904, w. 20cm. (Sandy Stanley)

1.180 Orion pewter mounted glass vase with cherry motif c.1905, h. 10cm. The glass is possibly Val St Lambert. (FCR Gallery London)

1.181 Orion Pewter and crystal Art Nouveau claret jug c.1904, h. 28cm. (Didier Antiques)

1.182 Orion pewter mounted glass butter dish (model 219) designed by Friedrich Adler c.1904, w. 19cm. (Quintys)

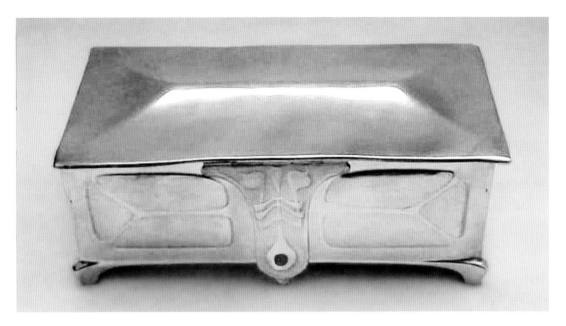

1.183 Orion pewter box probably designed by Friedrich Adler c.1905,
w. 17cm. This piece is unmarked and has been stylistically attributed to Orion.
(FCR Gallery London)

1.184 Orion pewter and oak tea set (models 200-203) designed by
Friedrich Adler c.1905, coffee pot: h. 24cm. (Private Collection, London)

Examples of Orion Marks

Other German Firms
1900 – 1930

The international success of commercial metalware firms in Germany such as WMF, Kayserzinn, Orivit and Osiris prompted many other smaller firms to produce quality Jugendstil goods in pewter.

DARMSTADT ARTIST COLONY AND THE DEUTSCHER WERKBUND

Germany was undeniably experiencing a renaissance of art and culture at the end of the 19th century. In 1899 the Darmstadt artist colony was founded and it included the prominent designers and architects Peter Behrens (1868-1940), Albin Müller (1871-1941), Paul Bürck (1878-1947), Rudolf Bosselt (1871-1938), Hans Christiansen (1866-1945), Ludwig Habich (1872-1949), Patriz Huber (1878-1902) and Joseph Maria Olbrich (1867-1908). The Deutscher Werkbund, formed in Munich in 1907, was another cluster of like minded individuals. These groups unified art, design and architecture – a concept that would carry on throughout the 20th century and be perpetuated via the Bauhaus and the Modernist movement. The Deutscher Werkbund comprised architects and designers: Peter Behrens, Theodor Fischer (1862-1938), Bruno Paul (1874-1968), Richard Riemerschmid (1868-1957) and Josef Hoffmann (1870-1956).

Both of these important groups created a hothouse for industrial design in Germany which is still evident today. The British Arts & Crafts movement, championed by Hermann Muthesius,[1] influenced these groups and many chose to work in pewter; examples of Olbrich, Behrens, Albin Müller, Patriz Huber and Richard Gross proliferate and some are illustrated in the following pages. One of the earliest examples of German Jugendstil pewter appears in *The Studio* in 1899. It was designed by Richard Gross and was fashioned using traditional repousse techniques rather than being moulded (see Plate 1.185).

EDWARD HUECK

The firm of Edward Hueck was founded around 1900 by the grandsons of a button-maker who transformed the family business into a flourishing manufacturer of fine

1.185 German repousse pewter charger from the early 20th century by Richard Gross and executed by L. Lichtinger depicting wheat sheaths in the Art Nouveau style c.1900, size unknown. (*The Studio*, vol 16)

artistic pewterware. Hueck is best known for the many items modelled by notable designers Albin Müller, Peter Behrens and Joseph Maria Olbrich (Plate 1.187).

GERHARDI & CO.

Gerhardi & Co. made quality pewterware from the mid-19th century. Under the direction of Carl Stienweg, the company moved into Jugendstil design commissioning models from such notable designers as Albert Reimann (Plate 1.195), Albin Müller, Olbrich, Behrens, and the French designer Maurice Dufrene.

ALBERT REIMANN

Albert Reimann set up his own workshop in Berlin producing a range of artistic pewter. In 1901, three of his items were chosen for reproduction in *The Studio* (Plates 1.221 and 1.222). They are described as 'excellent decorative designs utilising a new type of tin-metal called Kayserzinn which has the advantage of being indestructible and does not scratch like silver'.[2]

---

1. Adam Gottlieb Hermann Muthesius, also known as Hermann Muthesius (1861-1927) was a German architect and author who worked as a diplomat in England and was inspired by the English Arts & Crafts movement. He wrote books on the subject of 'The English Home' and later exported these philosophies to his native Germany.

2. *The Studio* magazine, 1901, vol 24, pages 65-66.

1.186 Edward Hueck pewter schnapps beaker designed by Albin Müller c.1901, h. 8.5cm. This is marked with the A.M. monogram and also with the Hueck silberzinn mark. (Collection Paul Weatherall)

DAUTZENBERG AND B&G IMPERIAL ZINN

Franz Xaver Dautzenberg and Peter Bitter created Dautzenberg in 1899. Dautzenberg created a number of stylised high Art Nouveau objects including monumental vases designed by J.R. Hannig and Alphonse Piquemal, a Belgian sculptor (Plate 1.209).

In 1899 Peter Bitter also founded B&G Imperial Zinn with Kaufmann Wilhelm Gobbers. The company made significant pewter objects including elaborate candelabra designed by the French sculptor Maurel. Other quality items for the desk and table were popular and exported all over Europe. The creative team worked in both the high Art Nouveau style, with flowing maiden designs, and in the more geometric Secessionist style. The output was of a high standard, although rarely cutting edge (Plates 1.201, 1.203 and 1.204). It is possible that they also marked some of their pieces as Kayser with an eagle mark.

These two companies were interchangeable in many ways, both in terms of direction and taste.

HANS PETER – FABRIK FEINER METALLWAREN

Hans Peter was the creator of a number of fine Jugendstil items and he worked for WMF before setting out on his own. His firm, Fabrik Feiner Metallwaren, was founded in Esslingen in 1902 and known as Württemberger Alfenidwerke from 1908 and produced a range of pewter called Juventa Prima Metal.[3] It is not known why he chose an Italian sounding name for the line of products – perhaps it was due to the romantic connotations. In the past it has been thought that Jeuventa was a Dutch firm, but Graham Dry's observations in *The Modern Art Of Metalwork* dispute this and further evidence is presented by two pewter mounted Loetz vases, one marked 'Juventa Prima Metal', the other marked 'Royal-Zinn HP' (Plate 1.219).

DEFFNER

Another Esslingen factory of note was Deffner, founded in 1824. The factory produced a vast array of items in the Art Nouveau style. Deffner hired skilled designers and, although they are best known for their output in brass and copper, a number of interesting pewter models were also manufactured (Plates 1.224 and 1.225).

F. VAN HAUTEN & SPRINGMANN

In the early 1890s F. van Hauten & Springmann of Bonn began to work in the Art Nouveau style. They produced a variety of stylish pewter vases, bowls and card trays (Plates 1.231, 1.232, 1.233, 1.234 and 1.235). Their most sought after items combined Loetz and Kralik glass, as well as ceramic vessels by Villeroy & Boch, set in organic pewter mounts. The firm exhibited at a number of important trade fairs including the 1904 World Exhibition in St. Louis.

BAUHAUS

Many of the smaller German metalwork factories ceased trading around the time of the First World War and then in the inter-war years much of the innovative production shifted to Weimar. In 1919. The architect Walter Gropius founded a new school aptly named Bauhaus (or 'Building School'). It inspired and continues to inspire modern design as we know it. The main metalwork teachers and designers at Bauhaus were Marianne Brandt, Christian Dell and Karl Raichle. They mostly worked in silver, brass and steel, however some commercially manufactured designs were fashioned in pewter, steel and tin (Plates 1.239, 1.240 and 1.241).

3. *The Modern Art Of Metalware*, Brohan quoting Graham Dry p. 256.

1.187 Edward Hueck copper electroplated coffee pot (model 1950) designed by Peter Behrens c.1904, h. 25cm. (FCR Gallery London)

1.188 Chalice with green glass cabochon probably designed by Friedrich Adler c.1905, h. 23cm. This piece is unmarked and has been stylistically attributed to Orion. (FCR Gallery London)

1.189 Gerhardi & Co. pewter sugar bowl designed by Albin Müller c.1902, d. 12.5cm. (Sandy Stanley)

1.190 Pewter Art Nouveau fruit bowl designed by Hugo Leven c.1906, h. 29.5cm, w. 41.5cm, signed on bowl. (Titus Omega)

1.191 Pewter box in the style of J.M. Olbrich. This box was possibly manufactured by Gerhardi & Co. c.1900, w. 15cm. (FCR Gallery London)

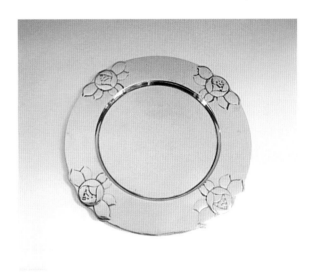

1.192 Edward Hueck small pewter dish (model 1861) designed by J.M. Olbrich c.1902, d. 13cm. (So-Nouveau)

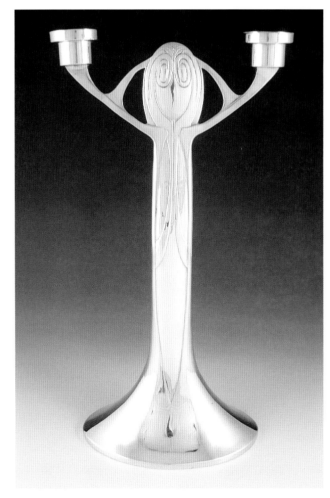

1.193 Edward Hueck pewter candelabrum (model 1819) designed by J.M. Olbrich c.1902, h. 36cm. (Titus Omega)

1.194 Edward Hueck pewter plate (model 1820) designed by J.M. Olbrich c.1902, d. 30cm. (FCR Gallery London)

1.196 German pewter candelabrum possibly by Hans Peter c.1900, h. 38cm, indistinct mark: 'TF'. (Hall-Bakker)

1.195 Gerhardi & Co. pewter candelabra (model 447) designed by Albert Reimann c.1902, h. 38.5cm. (Titus Omega)

1.197 Dautzenberg pewter and uranium glass schnapps set c.1900,
h. 12cm. (FCR Gallery London)

1.198 Dautzenberg pewter mounted glass
claret jug c.1900, h. 40cm.
(FCR Gallery London)

1.199 Bingit Zinn pewter schnapps set c.1905, h. 20cm. (Titus Omega)

1.200 B&G Imperial (Bitter & Gobbers) GMBH pewter & enamel tazza
c.1903, h. 26cm. (FCR Gallery London)

1.201 B&G Imperial (Bitter & Gobbers) pewter with ceramic plaque clock
1904, h. 21cm. (Collection Sergei Glebov)

1.202 B&G Imperial (Bitter &
Gobbers) dish with blue enamel
plaque 1904, w. 15cm.
(FCR Gallery London)

1.203 Imperial Zinn pewter inkwell fashioned as a racing car c.1905, w. 31cm. (Titus Omega)

1.204 B&G Imperial Zinn pewter and enamel inkstand c.1902, w. 20cm. (FCR Gallery London)

1.205 Pewter gilt mirror probably designed by Hans Peter unsigned c.1903, h. 23cm. (Sandy Stanley)

1.206 Juventa pewter maiden visiting card tray c.1902, h. 16cm. (FCR Gallery London)

1.207 Juventa dish with maiden motif c.1900, d. 21cm. (FCR Gallery London)

1.208 Unmarked German gilt pewter character jug depicting Kaiser Wilhelm II, c.1905, h. 20cm. (FCR Gallery London)

1.209 Dautzenberg pewter figural jardinière designed by Piquemal c.1902, h. 30cm. (FCR Gallery London)

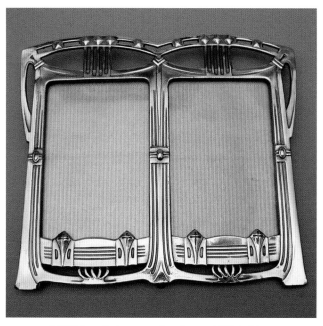

1.210 Secessionist pewter photo frame c.1905, h. 14cm.
(FCR Gallery London)

1.211 German pewter Art Nouveau photo frame, unmarked c.1903, h. 20cm.
(FCR Gallery London)

1.212 German pewter Art Nouveau photo frame with maiden, unmarked
c.1903, h. 20cm. (FCR Gallery London)

1.213 German pewter Art Nouveau photo frame, unmarked c.1903, h. 20cm.
(FCR Gallery London)

1.214 Unmarked German pewter and crystal
centrepiece with Mucha style maiden c.1902, w. 30cm.
(FCR Gallery London)

1.215 Unmarked German pewter crystal and
green cabochon vase c.1905, h. 20cm.
(FCR Gallery London)

1.216 Dautzenberg monumental German pewter vase
designed by J. Rob Hannig c.1900,
h. 60cm. (Titus Omega)

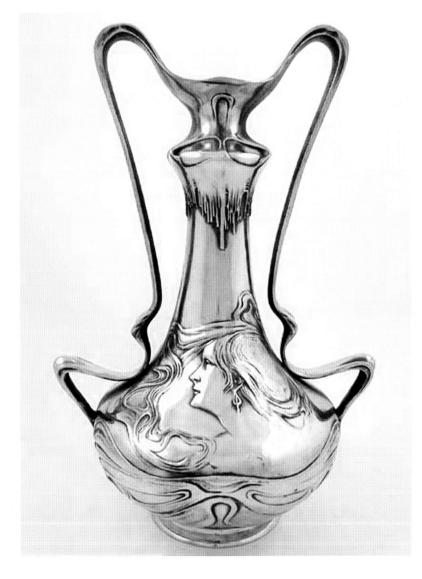

1.217 Dautzenberg German pewter vase designed by
J. Rob Hannig c.1900, h. 40cm. (So-Nouveau)

1.218 A pewter Art Nouveau figural vase attributed to Kayser, c.1902, h. 35cm. (Titus Omega)

1.219 Royal Zinn Art Nouveau pewter mounted Loetz glass vase designed by
Hans Peter c.1902, h. 31cm. This vase was made using Loetz blanks in gold,
green and cobalt blue papillon pattern glass. The vase is marked with both the
Royal Zinn logo and HP for Hans Peter.
(FCR Gallery London)

1.220 Large Imperial Zinn gilt pewter Art Nouveau lamp c.1906,
h. 43cm. (FCR Gallery London)

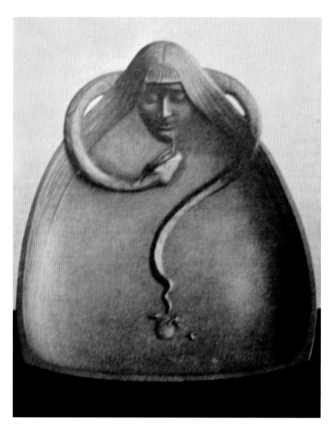

1.221 Albert Reimann pewter *vide poche* depicting a woman and serpent illustrated in *The Studio* 1901, w. 10cm. (*The Studio*, vol 24, 1901, p.65-6)

1.222 Albert Reimann pewter vide poche depicting a mermaid woman and serpent. illustrated in *The Studio*, 1901, w. 15cm. (*The Studio*, vol 24, 1901, p.65-6)

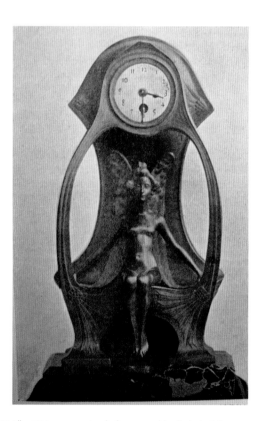

1.223 Albert Reimann pewter clock on a marble plinth depicting a sensuous fairy. Illustrated in *The Studio*, 1901, h. 36cm. (*The Studio*, vol 24, 1901, p.65-6)

1.224 Deffner pewter and cut crystal Art Nouveau jug c.1904, h. 30cm. (Didier Antiques)

106

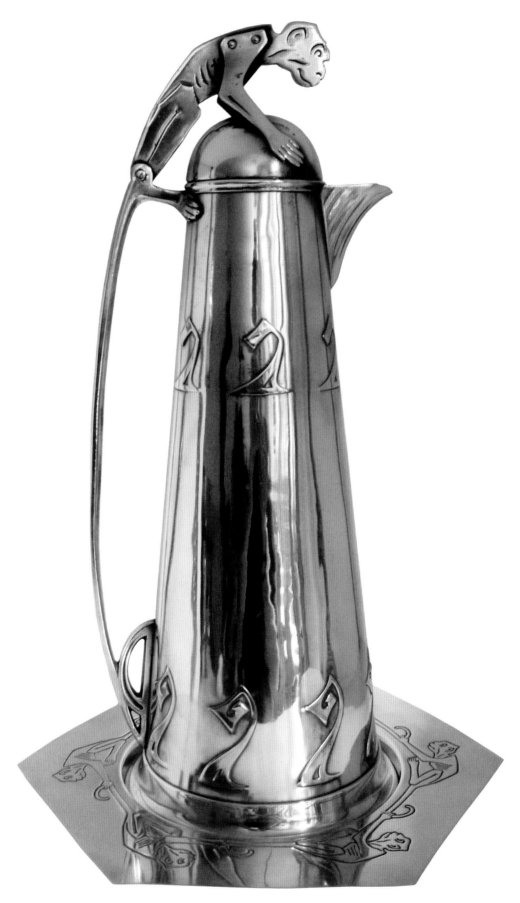

1.225 Deffner pewter and brass jug and tray with novelty monkey handle c.1904, h. 36cm. (FCR Gallery London)

1.226 Kayser pewter mounted clock c.1900, 20cm height.
(Quinty's Art Nouveau)

1.227 Kayser pewter ink stand modelled as an Art Nouveau maiden c.1900, w. 23cm. (FCR Gallery London)

1.228 Kayser pewter jug c.1904, h. 35cm. (Sandy Stanley)

1.230 Kayser pewter calling card tray with secessionist maiden, unmarked, c.1904, w. 20cm. (So-Nouveau)

1.229 Kayser Pewter jewel box with peacock motif c.1904, w. 18cm. (FCR Gallery London)

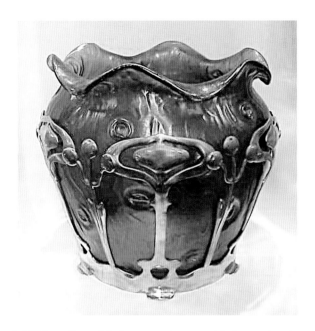

1.231 F. van Hauten & Springmann pewter mounted Rusticana pattern Loetz vase c.1903, h. 23cm. (FCR Gallery London)

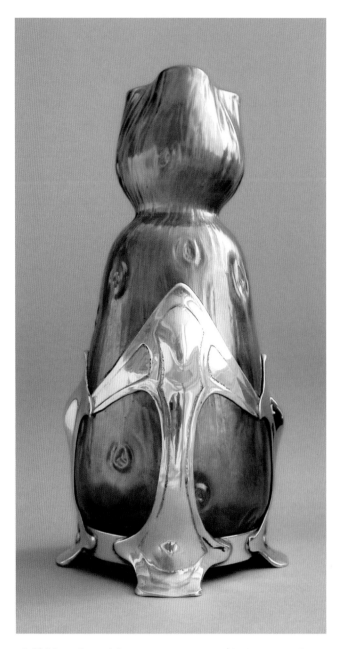

1.233 F. van Hauten & Springmann pewter mounted Rusticana pattern Loetz vase c.1903, h. 28cm. (FCR Gallery London)

1.232 Johanne von Schwarz (attributed) pewter mounted ceramic vase, h. 21cm. It is possible that the pewter mount was made by F. van Hauten & Springmann, who bought in ceramic blanks from the J. von Schwarz workshop in Nuremberg. (Private Collection London)

1.234 F. van Hauten & Springmann pewter mounted Loetz bowl c.1903,
d 22cm. (FCR Gallery London)

1.235 F. van Hauten & Springmann pewter mounted Rusticana pattern Loetz
vase c.1903, h. 16cm. (FCR Gallery London)

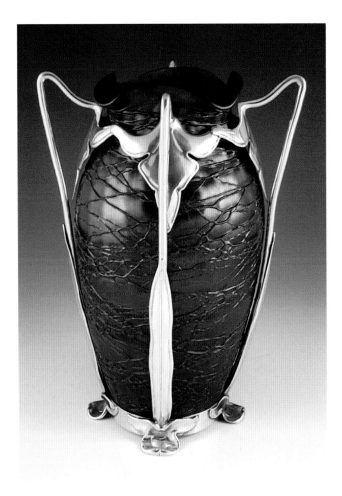

1.236 F. van Hauten & Springmann pewter mounted Pallme Konig vase c.1905, h. 28cm. (Titus Omega)

1.237 F. van Hauten & Springmann pewter mounted Pallme Konig vase c.1905, h. 19cm. (Titus Omega)

1.238 Hand-wrought pewter candelabra designed by Karl Raichle for Meersburger Zinnschmiede c.1933, w. 32cm. (Photo: George Shoterioo Servus Kunst)

1.239 Christian Dell for Kaiser (model 6556) steel and tin desk lamp c.1930, h. 43cm. (FCR Gallery London)

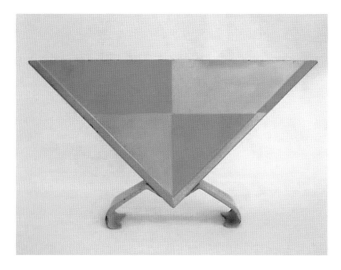

1.240 Marianne Brandt blue napkin stand for Ruppelwerk c.1930, h. 13.5cm. (FCR Gallery London)

1.241 Marianne Brandt yellow napkin stand for Ruppelwerk c.1930, h. 13.5cm. (FCR Gallery London)

Examples of Makers' Marks

Hueck mark with Joseph Maria Olbrich monogram

Gerhardi & Cie

Albin Müller monogram

Alphonse Piquemal

Bingit Zinn

Juventa

B&G Imperial

Kayser

Eduard Hueck

F.X. Dautzenberg

Carl Ulrich Christian Deffner

J.R. Hannig

J.R. Hannig

Royal Zinn with Hans Peter initials

Ruppelwerk

BRITISH PEWTER

Liberty & Co Pewter

The name of Liberty & Co has represented a high standard of quality for over a century. Arthur Lasenby Liberty founded this great London emporium in 1875, mainly specialising in fine imported silk and oriental ceramics. His Regent Street shop became popular with the aesthetes of the period attracting such notable painters as Dante Gabriel Rossetti (1828-1882) and Edward Burne-Jones (1833-1898). The Pre-Raphaelite painters were always searching for interesting fabrics to use as backdrops in their paintings and Liberty's proved a rich source of inspiration.

Arthur Liberty had keen business acumen and was also a master at marketing. The rise of Liberty's popularity can be linked to its ability to capture the public's changing mood and taste at a time when England was reaping the financial benefits of the Industrial Revolution and the expansive British Empire.

In the late 19th century there was a resurgence of craft guilds in Britain. These workshops tried to emulate the guilds of the Middle Ages. Many were moderately successful and set up their own shops or found more established retailers such as Morris & Co to sell their wares. All items were hand made and lovingly crafted. This era produced some of the finest objects seen since the Renaissance, but they were priced at a level that only a Medici could afford. Liberty was able to encapsulate the essence of this style, which became known as the Arts & Crafts Movement. He utilised modern methods of production and was a capable force in bringing this fashionable style to the masses at an affordable price.

Liberty began his infatuation with pewter at the turn of the 20th century. The revival of pewter as a medium for tableware and decorative objects was already popular in Germany and Liberty turned to companies such as Kayserzinn (Plate 1.84), Osiris and Orivit as a readily available source of ideas. It is also thought that Liberty

stocked items from WMF, the largest of the German pewter firms. The entire range proved to be extremely popular and pieces appeared in abundance in the Liberty Yuletide catalogues of the period. It was at this point that Liberty saw the commercial opportunity in manufacturing his own range of pewter.

Liberty had already established a partnership with W.H. Haseler, a silver workshop based in Birmingham, which produced a wide range of household silver items and jewellery, much of it enamelled. Many of these items were commission pieces and very expensive. Liberty financed the expansion of Haseler's workshop, which then developed the capacity to produce leadless pewter. This new type of pewter was made up of 94.6% tin, 4.2% antimony, 0.79% copper and 0.28% silver.[1] Liberty wanted to shed the Germanic influences of his pewter range and produce a pure British vernacular rival. He aptly named it Tudric, a title created to evoke the romance of the Tudor period.

The key to Liberty's success lay in his flare for recognising new and exciting design and, more pertinently, his hiring of top designers. One example of this was The Silver Studio, a family firm consisting of Arthur Silver and his sons Rex and Harry. Towards the end of the 19th century they produced some of the most vibrant fabric designs of the period.

Some of the earliest production pieces of Liberty pewter were based on designs by David Veasey, for example the rose bowl motto on Plate 2.42. The entry for a design of a motto bowl appears in a competition in *The Studio* c.1899. It is not known whether this drawing was purchased from the artist directly, but it is likely that it was Veasey's introduction to The Silver Studio, where he continued to work as a fabric designer into the 1920s.

Archibald Knox also started his relationship with Liberty & Co through The Silver Studio. Knox hailed from

---

1. This information was kindly provided by William Grant. It was carried out by the Sheffield Analytical Services and contradicts earlier information available in Mervyn Levy's book Liberty Style. It is interesting to note that silver was part of the alloys used, as 20th century pewter was often referred to as poor man's silver.

the Isle of Man where he attended Art College in the capital, Douglas. His native Celtic roots, inspired by a childhood fascination with local archaeology, heavily influenced his style. This can be clearly seen by his use of intertwining Celtic knots and indigenous plant motifs. Christopher Dresser, the father of Industrial Design, very likely employed Knox in the early days; it is a much-debated topic amongst design historians. Knox was certainly aware of Dresser's designs and published theories. His clean Modernist shapes, many designed around the time of Dresser's death, reflect this.

Liberty pewter was polished to give a bright silver finish. They added a planished effect to the surface of the pewter in the moulds, to give it a hand hammered finish. The first offerings, mainly candlesticks, bowls and vases, struck a note with the public and became a popular seller. The Liberty design department saw the commercial potential of adding handmade enamels to the moulded pewter and they headhunted C. R. Ashbee's main enamel designer, Charles Varley, from the Guild Of Handicraft's workshop. These enamels were mainly used to adorn pewter cigarette and jewellery boxes that were almost exact copies of the Guild's silver originals (Plates 2.86-2.90).

Another first wave pewter designer at Liberty was Oliver Baker (Plates 2.20 and 2.59). Baker's style was more traditional utilising design elements similar to W. A. S. Benson. This is evident in his use of splayed handles, strapping and pointed raised feet. His most unusual offering is a bowl which is of a shape inspired by an organic sea creature (Plate 2.41). It is slightly more Germanic in appearance than other Liberty designs and borrows from Hugo Leven, the Kayserzinn designer. Bernard Curzan was also commissioned to design for Liberty, although it is rare to find any of his work in pewter.

Liberty continued to produce pewter ware until the First World War, after which the style altered dramatically reflecting the new taste for anything Art Deco. These items were simple, plain or sometimes planished. Some items had narrow traditional border designs around the rims or bases. The earlier, more popular designs continued in production until the Second World War and, for variety, some of the smooth finished designs were recreated with a planished effect and enamelled buttons were added to update the models.

In many ways Liberty never regained its design edge after the First World War. It always remained a cutting edge retailer, mounting exciting exhibitions throughout the 20th century, but after the death of Arthur Liberty in 1917, the shop seemed to have lost its ability to actively create and market exciting, original designs.

Marks

Liberty pewter bears a number of different stamped marks. The most common are Tudric, English Pewter, Made for Liberty & Co and Carolean. Generally, a production number beginning with 0 follows. A number of different interpretations have been made as to the dating of these numbers. Mervyn Levy, in his book *Liberty Style*, states that the number 0370 would place the item in question at 1904/5. However, it is also logical that the 03 is the date and the 70 the actual production number.[2]

2. *Liberty Style*, Mervyn Levy, Rizzoli, 1986.

2.1 Liberty & Co. pewter enamel group designed by Archibald Knox c.1902-1905 including charger (model 0163), candlesticks (model 0223) and biscuit box (model 0194). (FCR Gallery London)

2.2 Liberty & Co. pewter and copper clock (model 0159) designed c.1902-1905, h. 16.5cm. The clock case was adapted from an original design for a biscuit box illustrated in *The Studio* magazine. (Titus Omega)

2.3 Liberty & Co. pewter with inset abalone wall clock designed by Archibald Knox 1905, h. 27cm. (Titus Omega)

2.4 Liberty & Co. pewter enamel clock with tree of life motif (model 01144) designed by David Veasey c.1902-1905, h. 19.5cm. This clock was a smaller example of an earlier design (model 0150). (Titus Omega)

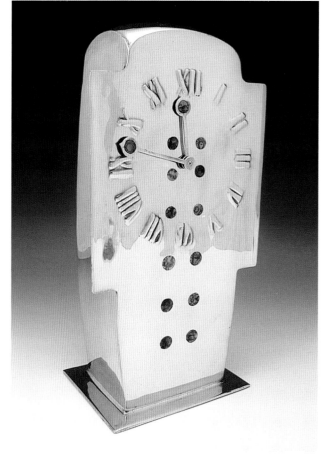

2.5 Liberty & Co. pewter with inset abalone clock (model 097) designed by Archibald Knox c.1902-1905, h. 37cm. This clock was inspired by traditional Manx Celtic Crosses. (Titus Omega)

2.6 Liberty & Co. pewter, abalone and enamel clock (model 0252) designed by
Archibald Knox c.1902-1905, h. 17cm. (Private Collection, London)

2.7 Liberty & Co. pewter and enamel clock (model 0609) designed by Archibald Knox c.1902, h. 20cm. (Titus Omega)

2.8 Liberty & Co. pewter mantle clock designed by Archibald Knox (model 0255) c.1902-1905, h. 23 cm. (Photo: Lyon & Turnbull)

2.9 Liberty & Co. pewter copper and enamel clock (model 0367) probably designed by Oliver Baker c.1903-5, h. 16cm. (FCR Gallery London)

2.10 Liberty & Co. pewter and enamel clock (model 0370) designed by Archibald Knox c.1902, h. 23cm. (FCR Gallery London)

2.11 Liberty & Co. pewter and enamel architectural clock (model 0629)
designed by Archibald Knox 1902-1905, h. 17.8cm. (FCR Gallery London)

2.12 Liberty & Co. pewter and enamel clock with Celtic knot (model 0978) in the Knox style, but probably designed by Rex Silver 1905-1906, h. 10cm. (FCR Gallery London)

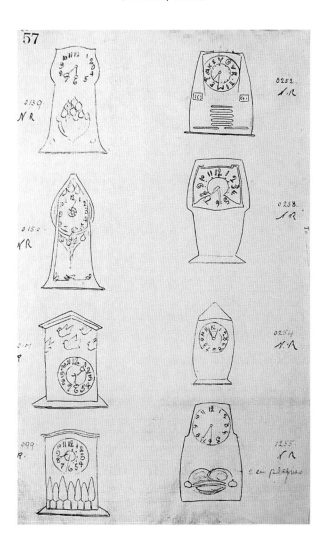

2.13 Liberty & Co. pewter and enamel clock with stylised tree motif (model 0371) designed by Rex Silver 1902-1905, h. 22.8cm. (FCR Gallery London)

2.15 Liberty & Co. pewter and James Powell glass jar designed by Archibald Knox c.1905, h. 13.5cm. (Titus Omega)

2.14 Liberty & Co. catalogue showing a page of clocks c.1901.

121

2.16 Liberty & Co. bowl (model 0964) designed by Archibald Knox c.1905,
h. 14.5cm. (Titus Omega)

2.17 Liberty & Co. pewter wine cooler (model 075) designed by Archibald
Knox c.1902-1905, h. 23 cm. (Collection Sergei Glebov)

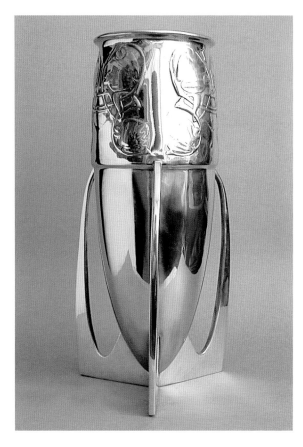

2.18 Liberty & Co. pewter ice bucket (model 0705) designed by
Archibald Knox c.1902-1905, h. 20cm. (FCR Gallery London)

2.19 Liberty & Co. pewter 'bomb' vase (model 0927) designed by Archibald Knox
c.1902, h. 29cm. (FCR Gallery London)

2.20 Liberty & Co. pewter and enamel tulip vases (model 029) designed by
Oliver Baker c.1903, h. 25cm. (FCR Gallery London)

2.21 Liberty & Co. pewter vase (model 0228) designed by Archibald Knox c.1902, h. 16cm. (FCR Gallery London)

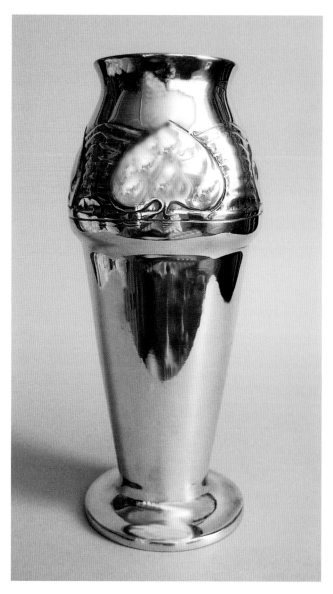

2.22 Liberty & Co. pewter vase (model 02510) with peacock motif designed by Rex Silver c.1905, h. 20cm. (FCR Gallery London)

2.23 Liberty & Co. vase (model 0820) with design by Archibald Knox c.1910, h. 15cm. (FCR Gallery London)

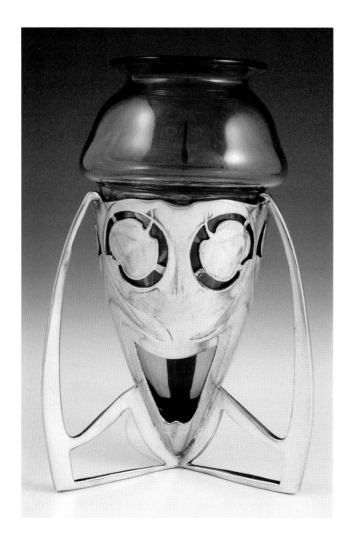

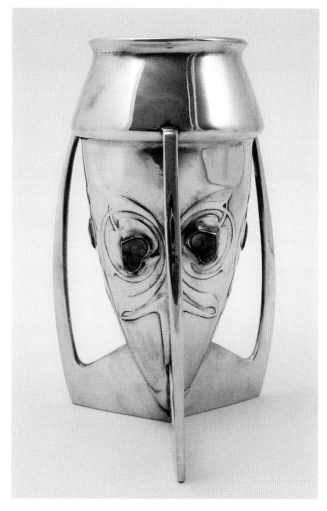

2.24 Liberty & Co. pewter mounted James Powell of Whitefriars 'bomb' vase, cut out variation (model 0226) designed by Archibald Knox c.1905, h. 17cm. (Titus Omega)

2.25 Liberty & Co. pewter enamel 'bomb' vase (model 0225) designed by Archibald Knox c.1902-1905, h. 19cm. (FCR Gallery London)

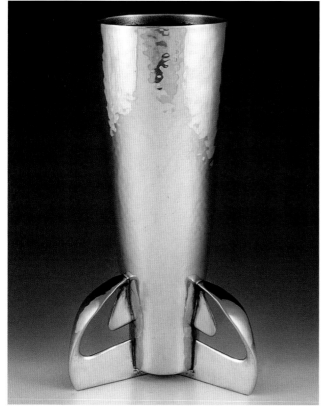

2.26 Liberty & Co. pewter vase (model 2187) designed by Archibald Knox. This vase was also manufactured with a floral pattern c.1902, h. 20cm. (Titus Omega)

2.27 Liberty & Co. pewter vase (model 0214) designed by Oliver Baker c.1902, h. 33.5cm. (Titus Omega)

2.28 Liberty & Co. pewter mounted Powell glass vase (model 0512) designed by Archibald Knox c.1902-1905, h. 15cm. (FCR Gallery London)

2.29 Liberty & Co. pewter mounted green glass vase (model 0324) designed by Archibald Knox c.1902-1905, h. 27.7cm. (FCR Gallery London)

2.31 Tudric Moorcroft vase, h. 18 cm. In the 1920s Liberty & Co. produced a range of pewter mounted Moorcroft pottery vases, tazzas and bowls. These are usually marked 'Tudric/Moorcroft'. (FCR Gallery London)

2.30 Liberty & Co. pewter loving cup (model 010) designed by David Veasey c.1901 with motto 'For Old Time's Sake', h. 24cm. (FCR Gallery London)

2.32 Liberty & Co. pewter candlesticks (model 023) designed by Archibald Knox c.1902, h. 12cm. (FCR Gallery London)

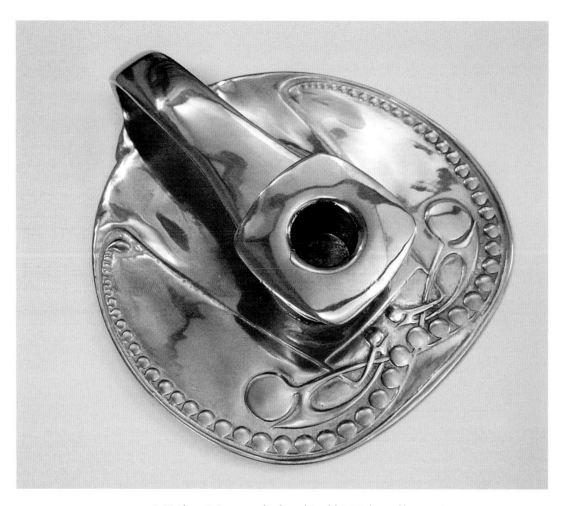

2.33 Liberty & Co. pewter chamberstick (model 0523) designed by
Archibald Knox c.1905, 16.6cm. (FCR Gallery London)

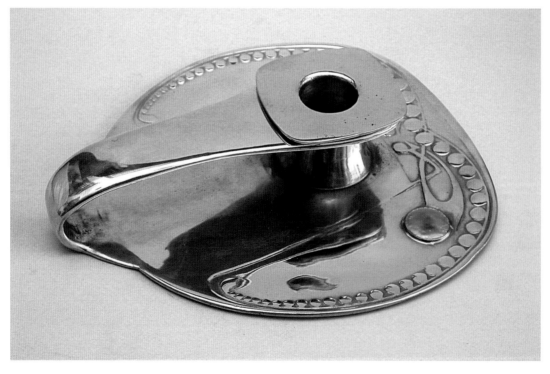

2.34 Liberty & Co. pewter and enamel chamberstick (model 0523) designed
by Archibald Knox c.1905, d. 13cm. (FCR Gallery London)

2.35 Liberty & Co. pewter candlesticks (model 0222) designed by
Archibald Knox c.1902, h. 9.5cm. (FCR Gallery London)

2.36 Liberty & Co. pewter candlesticks Celtic knot motif (model 08) Designed
by Archibald Knox c.1902, h.18cm. (FCR Gallery London)

2.37 Liberty & Co. pewter and enamel candlesticks (model 022) designed by
Archibald Knox c.1902, h. 12.3cm. (FCR Gallery London)

2.38 Liberty & Co. pewter enamel candlesticks (model 0223) designed by Archibald Knox c.1902-1905, h. 23.8cm. (FCR Gallery London)

2.40 Liberty & Co. pewter and abalone candlesticks (model 0725) designed by Archibald Knox c.1902, h. 31.5cm. (Collection Sergei Glebov)

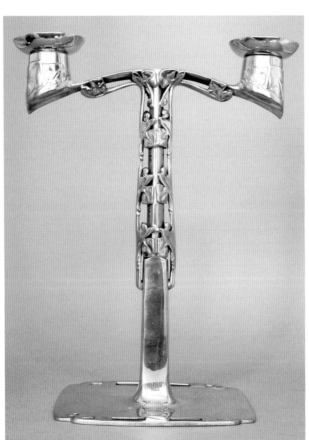

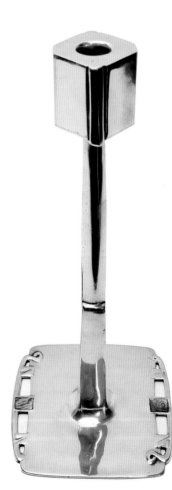

2.39 Liberty & Co. pewter twin branch candelabra (model 0530) designed by Archibald Knox c.1902-1905, h. 23.8cm. (FCR Gallery London)

2.41 Liberty & Co. pewter bowl (model 01029) designed by Oliver Baker
c.1906, d. 28cm. (FCR Gallery London)

2.42 Liberty & Co. pewter motto rose bowl (model 011) designed by
David Veasey c.1900, d. 23.5cm. This was one of the earliest and most
successful production pieces retailed by Liberty. The bowl features a quote by
Lord Alfred Tennyson: 'And the woodbine spices are wafted abroad and the
musk of the roses blown'. It was produced from an award winning competition
design featured in *The Studio* magazine c.1900. It is known that Veasey
continued to design for Liberty through the 1920s. (FCR Gallery London)

2.43 Liberty & Co. pewter and Clutha glass rose bowl (model 0276) designed
by Archibald Knox c.1902-1905, h. 17cm. (FCR Gallery London)

2.44 Liberty & Co. pewter mounted Clutha glass bowl designed by
Archibald Knox for Liberty & Co. c.1902-1905, h. 10cm. (FCR Gallery London)

2.45 Liberty & Co. pewter and enamelled rose bowl (model 0755) designed
by Archibald Knox 1902-1905, h. 15cm. (FCR Gallery London)

2.46 Liberty & Co. pewter rose bowl lined with green glass, probably designed by Rex Silver, incorporating David Veasey design elements borrowed from the Woodbine rose bowl (model 01), 1905, d. 23.5cm. (Titus Omega)

2.47 Liberty & Co. pewter enamelled rose bowl, with James Powell glass liner, (model 0230) designed by Archibald Knox 1902-1905, d. 30cm. (FCR Gallery London)

2.48 Liberty & Co. pewter and James Powell enamelled rose bowl (model 0320) designed by Archibald Knox 1902-1905, d. 20.4cm. (FCR Gallery London)

2.49 Liberty & Co. pewter and James Powell bowl (model 0924) designed by Archibald Knox 1902-1905, d. 20cm. (Titus Omega)

2.50 Liberty & Co. pewter and enamel rose bowl (model 0229) designed by Archibald Knox 1902-1905. (FCR Gallery London)

2.51 Liberty & Co. large pewter rose bowl (model 0788) designed by Oliver Baker 1905, d. 29cm. (Titus Omega)

2.52 Liberty & Co. pewter and enamel jardinière (model 0864) designed by Rex Silver 1905, h. 17cm. (FCR Gallery London)

2.53 Liberty & Co. pewter bowl (model 0277) designed by Archibald Knox 1902-1905, h. 9cm. (FCR Gallery London)

2.54 Liberty & Co. pewter and enamel tankard (model 0305) designed by Archibald Knox 1902-1905, h. 20cm. (FCR Gallery London)

2.55 Liberty & Co. pewter and enamel tankard (model 0334) designed by Archibald Knox 1902-1905, h. 13.2cm. (FCR Gallery London)

2.57 Liberty & Co. large pewter and enamel lidded flagon (model 053) this tankard incorporates a CFA Voysey inspired design with tree of life motif. 1902-1905, h. 35.7cm. (Titus Omega)

2.56 Liberty & Co. pewter and James Powell glass decanter (model 0229) designed by Archibald Knox 1902-1905, h. 20.5cm. (Titus Omega)

2.58 Liberty & Co. pewter lidded tankard (model 0335) designed by Archibald Knox 1902-1905, h. 15.5cm. (FCR Gallery London)

2.59 Liberty & Co. pewter tankard (model 066) designed by Oliver Baker 1902, h. 14cm. This early tankard was produced in half pint and pint sizes and proved so popular that it was in production until the 1930s. (FCR Gallery London)

2.60 Liberty & Co. pewter and enamel lidded tankard (model 0064) designed by Archibald Knox 1902-1905, h. 14cm. (FCR Gallery London)

2.61 Liberty & Co. Large pewter flagon (model 0304) designed by Archibald Knox 1902-1905, h. 35cm. (Titus Omega)

2.62 Liberty & Co. pewter and enamel inkstand (model 0715) designed by
Archibald Knox 1902-1905, w. 26cm. (Titus Omega)

2.63 Liberty & Co. pewter and enamel inkstand (model 0404) designed by
Archibald Knox 1902-1905, w. 23.8cm. (FCR Gallery London)

2.64 Liberty & Co. pewter and enamel inkwell (model 0141) designed by
Archibald Knox 1902-1905, h. 10cm. (FCR Gallery London)

2.65 Liberty & Co. pewter and enamel dish (model 0287) designed by
Rex Silver c.1904, w. 23cm. (FCR Gallery London)

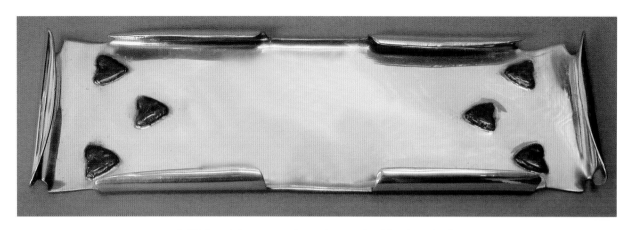

2.66 Liberty & Co. pewter and enamel pen tray (model not known) with
Voysey heart motif. 1902-1905, w. 20cm. (FCR Gallery London)

2.67 Liberty & Co. pewter pepper pot (model 0348)
designed by Archibald Knox 1902-1905, h. 6cm.
(Paul Weatherall)

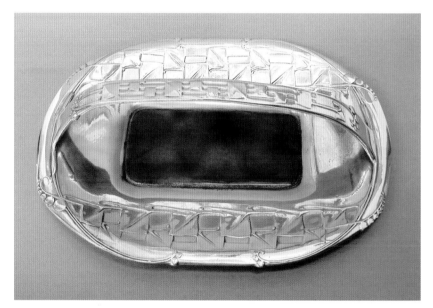

2.68 Liberty & Co. pewter and enamel cake basket (model 0357) designed by
Archibald Knox 1902-1905. w. 30.7cm. (FCR Gallery London)

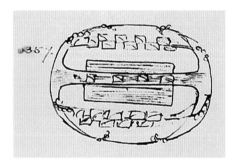

2.69 Original drawing from the Liberty sketchbook
c.1902.

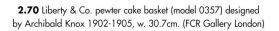

2.70 Liberty & Co. pewter cake basket (model 0357) designed
by Archibald Knox 1902-1905, w. 30.7cm. (FCR Gallery London)

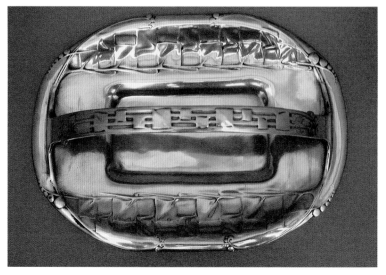

2.71 Liberty & Co. pewter and enamel biscuit box (model 0194) designed by Archibald Knox 1902-1905 h. 14.2cm. (FCR Gallery London)

2.72 Liberty & Co. pewter and glass tobacco jar c.1920, h. 18cm. The glass was most like manufactured by Stourbridge. Marked 'Liberty'. (FCR Gallery London)

2.73 Liberty & Co. pewter biscuit box with stylised honesty pattern (model 0237) designed by Archibald Knox 1902-1905, h. 14.5cm. (FCR Gallery London)

2.74 Liberty & Co. pewter, glass lined, butter dish (model 0162) designed by Archibald Knox 1902-1905, d. 14.3cm. (FCR Gallery London)

2.75 Libery & Co. pewter photograph frame (model 0564) c.1905, 14 x 12.5cm (FCR Gallery London)

2.76 Liberty & Co. pewter photo frame (model 0229) designed by Archibald Knox 1902-1905, 18 x 18cm. (Titus Omega)

2.77 Liberty & Co. pewter photo frame (model 0109) designed by Archibald Knox 1902-1905, h. 19.2cm. This frame was also manufactured in silver. (FCR Gallery London)

2.78 Liberty & Co. pewter with abalone photo frame c.1902, w. 15cm. (Collection Sergei Glebov)

2.79 Liberty & Co., 'The Bollellin', a tray in pewter and enamel (model 044) polished designed by Archibald Knox 1902-1905, h. 25.4cm, polished. (FCR Gallery London)

2.81 Detail of 'The Bollellin' tray (model 044) with a Moorcroft Pottery insert. This was a later, hammered version of this well known tray c.1920. (FCR Gallery London)

2.80 Liberty & Co., 'The Bollellin', a tray in pewter and enamel (model 044) designed by Archibald Knox 1902-1905, h. 25.4cm, unpolished. (FCR Gallery London)

2.82 Liberty & Co. pewter and enamel charger
(model 0163) designed by Archibald Knox
1902-1905, d. 24.9cm. (FCR Gallery London)

2.83 Liberty & Co. pewter charger with green
cabochons (model 09) designed by Archibald Knox
1902-1905, d. 25cm. (Collection Sergei Glebov)

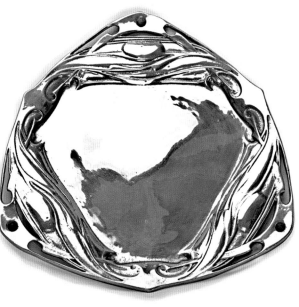

2.85 Liberty & Co. pewter and turquoise box designed by Rex Silver 1905,
w. 26cm. (Titus Omega)

2.84 Liberty & Co. pewter peacock charger (model 0114) designed by
Rex Silver 1902-1905 d. 32cm. The design on the roundels was also used as
a button design. (Titus Omega)

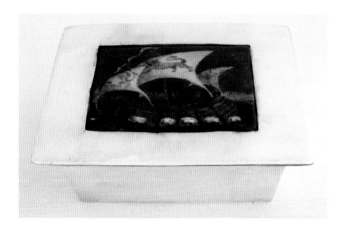

2.86 Liberty & Co. pewter box with enamel plaque depicting a galleon c.1905, w. 12.5cm. (FCR Gallery London)

Fleetwood Charles Varley was one of the most prominent enamel artists of the period. He began his career working for C.R. Ashbee's Guild Of Handicrafts, moving to Liberty & Co. around 1905. His sensitive handling of landscape painting, especially water and reflections, is unsurpassed.

2.87 Liberty & Co. pewter and enamel jewel box with plaque depicting sailboats at sunset 1908, w. 17cm. (FCR Gallery London)

2.88 Liberty & Co. pewter and enamel box with plaque by Fleetwood Charles Varley depicting a country lane c.1907, w. 17cm. (FCR Gallery London)

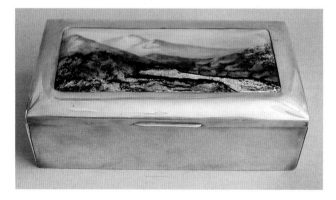

2.89 Liberty & Co. pewter and enamel box with plaque by Fleetwood Charles Varley depicting mountains and a river c.1908 W 17cm. FCR Gallery London)

2.90 Liberty & Co. pewter and enamel box with plaque by Fleetwood Charles Varley depicting a river in summer landscape1905, w. 10cm. (FCR Gallery London)

2.91 Liberty & Co. pewter and enamel box (model 0405) plaque with butterfly
motif 1905, w. 8.5cm. (FCR Gallery London)

2.92 Liberty & Co. pewter-covered muffin dish (model 0293) designed by
Archibald Knox 1902-1905, d. 25cm. (FCR Gallery London)

2.93 Liberty & Co. pewter and enamel tazza (model 0716) designed by
Archibald Knox 1902-1905, h. 27.5cm. This was most likely produced post
1910 as a centrepiece to complement the popular candlesticks (model 0223).
(FCR Gallery London)

2.94 Liberty & Co. pewter four-piece tea set with tray (model 0231) designed by Archibald Knox 1902-1905, w. 23.3cm. (FCR Gallery London)

2.95 Pewter tea set designed in the style of CFA Voysey (model 030) c.1901, teapot h. 23cm. (FCR Gallery London)

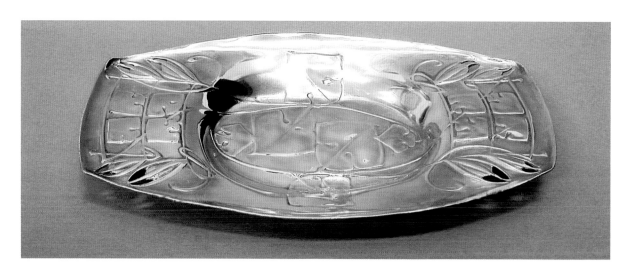

2.96 Liberty & Co. pewter pin tray (model 0547) designed by Archibald Knox
1902-1905, w. 23.2cm. (FCR Gallery London)

2.97 Liberty & Co. pewter 'slops bowl' (model 0231) designed by
Archibald Knox 1902-1905, w. 14cm. (FCR Gallery London)

2.98 Liberty & Co. pewter tray (model 0309) designed by Archibald Knox
1902-1905, w. 46cm. (FCR Gallery London)

2.99 pewter tray (model 0311) designed by Archibald Knox c.1902,
w. 35.6cm. (FCR Gallery London)

2.100 Liberty & Co. pewter tray (model 037) designed by Archibald Knox
1902-1905, w. 46cm. (Titus Omega)

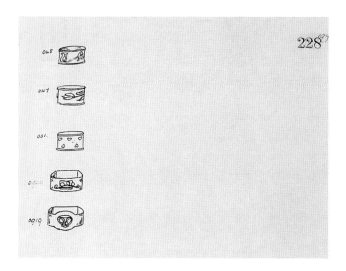

2.101 Page from Liberty sketchbook showing napkin rings.

2.102 Liberty & Co. pewter and enamel napkin ring (model 0920) designed
by Archibald Knox c.1902 w. 6cm. (FCR Gallery London)

2.103 Liberty & Co. pewter and enamel napkin ring (model number not
known) designed by Rex Silver c.1902, w. 6cm. (FCR Gallery London)

2.104 Liberty & Co. pewter knife rests designed by Archibald Knox c.1902, w. 9cm. (Titus Omega)

2.105 Liberty & Co. pewter knife rests designed by Archibald Knox c.1902, w. 9cm (Lyon & Turnbull)

2.106 Pewter wall mirror designed by Archibald Knox for Liberty & Co. c.1903, 72cm x 46cm. (Photo: Lyon & Turnbull)

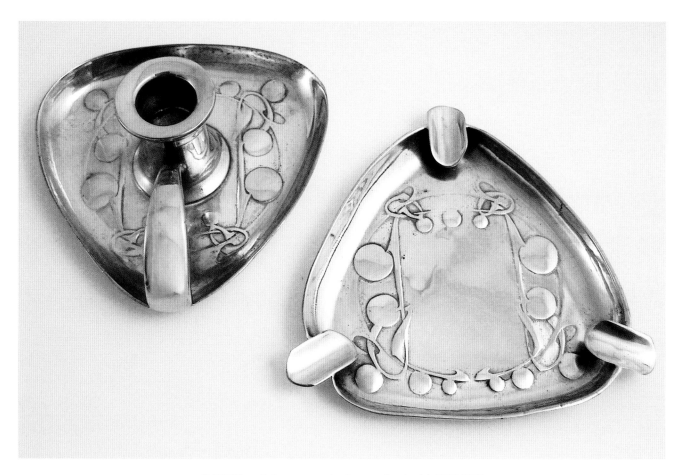

2.107 Liberty & Co. pewter smokers' compendium (models 0897, 0898)
designed by Archibald Knox c.1902, d. 13cm. (FCR Gallery London)

Examples of Liberty & Co. Marks

Other British Firms

The impact of the Arts & Crafts movement on British taste was extensive. It inspired many aspects of decoration and was especially noticeable in metalware design. Hand crafted repousse pewter was particularly popular with evening classes and many examples of these crafts have survived in the form of boxes, chargers, mirrors and vases.

Pewter in England

Keswick

The Keswick School of Industrial Art encouraged local Cumbrian craftsmen to work in copper, brass and pewter producing simple yet highly sophisticated hand crafted items for the home. Canon and Edith Rawnsley founded the school in 1884 and by 1893 the school had moved into its own purpose built premises. Harold Stabler, one of the most influential twentieth-century British designers, joined KSIA in 1898 as a full time teacher. This had a significant impact on the house style that was to develop. Keswick items were sold through Morris & Co. and Liberty & Co. in London. *The Studio* magazine featured Keswick metalware in a number of issues, creating a strong demand for these quality items.

Hugh Wallis

Hugh Wallis (1871-1944) was a painter turned metalworker. He created a stylish range of items in his Cheshire workshop utilising a Dinanderie technique of inlaying pewter and silver into copper. All of the Wallis output is hand raised and finished. Most of the designs are simple with some floral and fish motifs typical of Arts & Crafts metalware of the period. His items are clearly marked with an H.W. monogram.

Pewter Inlaid Furniture

The architect Mackay Hugh Baillie Scott often used pewter as a material for inlay in his furniture production (Plate 2.125). This trend was commercially adapted by Liberty & Co.'s chief furniture designer, Leonard Wyburd, who produced tables, sideboards and clocks using pewter inlay. It was common for many of the pewter manufacturers to add a planished or hammered finish to the surface of items to give them a handmade appearance. The success of Liberty & Co.'s Tudric range of pewter inspired many companies to create their own original lines of Arts & Craft style pewter.

William Hutton of Sheffield

William Hutton of Sheffield produced a popular silver range, including exceptional pieces designed by Kate Harris. Some of these inspired items were also modified and produced in pewter (Plates 2.115 and 2.121). Hutton also purchased pewter moulds form the Dutch firm Urania. Some of the well known designs by Friedrich Adler were reissued in the UK and marked 'Urania Hutton Sheffield'.

Connell & Co. of Cheapside

Connell & Co. of Cheapside in London, were noted for creating quality Art Nouveau designs in silver and in pewter. It is evident that they were allowed to purchase many of the discontinued Liberty & Co. pewter moulds, which were then used to create a range marketed as Connell & Co Pewter. Many items still have feint original Liberty model marks including the stamp 'English Pewter, Tudric' or a Liberty model number.

James Dixon

James Dixon produced a limited range of pewter replicating some of their more popular silver designs including the exceptional Edward Spencer (1872-1938) style riveted candlesticks. These were marked 'Cornish Pewter', evoking a romantic quaintness associated with rural village life (Plate 2.110).

Ashberry Pewter

Ashberry Pewter was a commercial firm in Sheffield. They produced a range of planished tea sets, bowls and vases, many with genuine Ruskin inserts. The name Ashberry was most likely derived from C.R. Ashbee, the founder of the Guild Of Handicrafts.

Civic Pewter

Civic Pewter was another firm who manufactured a range of pewter similar to that of Ashberry, using enamelled plaques and Ruskin inserts to embellish their objects.

Castle Pewter

Castle Pewter produced a number of unusual mantle clocks with copper and enamelled dials. Many were planished and riveted during moulding to give them a handcrafted appearance (Plate 2.109).

Homeland Pewter

Homeland was the brand name used for a rage of pewter from W. & Co. They were known for simple planished bowls and tea sets some with faux riveting as decoration. The items were usually stamped 'Hand Beaten' even though the plenishing was moulded into the items.

Pewter in Scotland

In Scotland, Charles Rennie Mackintosh, Margaret Macdonald Mackintosh, Herbert McNair and Frances Macdonald McNair created beautiful repousse work using a form of sheet pewter. This was likely an alloy known as block tin, a white metal made from a tin base which was partially refined and contained small quantities of copper, lead, iron, and arsenic. The 'Glasgow Four' also used admiralty brass, a metal alloy of tin, copper and zinc, with not more than 5% or 6% of other metals. This material was traditionally used in the ship building industry and was therefore readily available in Glasgow. Admiralty brass was extremely hard and less malleable then pewter. Examples of their repousse work were incorporated into furniture or used as decorative plaques for the wall. Charles Rennie Mackintosh also designed a fireplace surround for the white room of Miss Cranston's Ingram Street tea room (one of his best known commissions) in sheet pewter made from tin and lead (Plate 2.142).

A.E. Taylor

Pewter was also a popular embellishment inlaid into the furniture of A.E. Taylor. It was used alongside exotic woods and abalone, highlighting decorative ornamentation and detailing.

Margaret Gilmour

Margaret Gilmour, one of the leading Glasgow girls, designed a large range of items in admiralty brass including mirrors, candlesticks inkwells and wall sconces. Her work often had enamelled plaques and Ruskin inserts, embellishing patterns of honesty and butterflies.

Talwin Morris

Another Scottish designer of note was the book designer Talwin Morris (1865-1911). Morris created a small number of plaques in brass and admiralty brass including the illustrated image (Plate 2.146), a panel which hung at his office at Blackie's Design.

Alexander Ritchie

Alexander Ritchie (1856-1941) was another craftsman working in pewter. He is best known for incorporating Celtic entrelac decoration into repousse pewter designs (Plate 2.148).

Art Deco and Modernism

Following the First World War, pewter production resumed in Great Britain. Many of the items made were now in the Art Deco style. Tea sets with stepped ziggurat shapes and odeon embellishments were manufactured by several British companies.

Cube Teapots Ltd.

Cube Teapots Ltd. created models of their famous tea sets in ceramic, silver-plate and planished and plain pewter. They made one of the most original designs of the period, a tea set originally designed by the entrepreneur Robert Crawford Johnson, who patented the Cube Teaset in 1917. The design was later used on the Queen Mary ocean liner where it received international exposure (Plates 2.134 and 2.135).

Harold Stabler

Harold Stabler was another well-established designer during the Arts & Crafts period. He now made the transition into the Art Deco style producing a number of items in pewter ranging from the highly stylised to quite simple geometric and traditional forms (Plates 2.130 and 2.131).

Charles Boyton

Charles Boyton (1885-1958), a well respected silversmith, also designed examples in pewter. Some of his designs for James Dixon & Sons are in the Arts & Crafts style and reminiscent of C. R. Ashbee (Plates 2.132 and 2.133).

2.108 Pewter and copper English Arts & Crafts clock c.1900, h. 30cm. (FCR Gallery London)

2.109 Castle Pewter Arts & Crafts clock c.1910, l. 34cm, h. 20cm. (FCR Gallery London)

2.110 James Dixon Cornish pewter candlesticks c.1910, h. 35cm. These candlesticks were successfully marketed by James Dixon in silver from 1899 onwards. They are stylistically similar to a design by Edward Spencer, one of the founders of the Artificers Guild. The candlesticks capture the ethos of the Arts & Crafts movement by replicating hand plenishing and rivets. (Photo: FCR Gallery London)

2.111 Ashberry planished pewter vase with Ruskin pottery cabochons c.1910, h. 23 cm. (Photo: FCR Gallery London)

2.112 Ashberry pewter footed bowl with Ruskin pottery cabochons c.1910, d. 20 cm. (Photo: FCR Gallery London)

2.113 Civic Pewter jardinière with Ruskin pottery cabochons c.1910, d. 25 cm. (Photo: FCR Gallery London)

2.114 Hutton Pewter jardinière with Ruskin Pottery cabochons, c.1908, h. 16.5 cm. (Photo: So-Nouveau)

2.115 Hutton Pewter jardinière with heart shape Ruskin Pottery cabochons c.1908, h. 18 cm. (Photo: FCR Gallery London)

2.116 Hutton Pewter spoon, likely to have been used as a jam spoon, c.1908, l. 14cm (Photo: Didier Antiques)

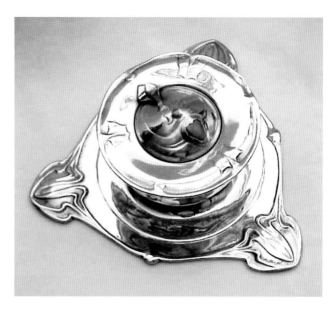

2.117 Hutton Inkwell with turquoise cabochons designed by Kate Harris c.1905, d. 12.5 cm. (Photo: FCR Gallery London)

2.118 Hutton Pewter ginger jar with blue Ruskin cabochons, c.1905, h. 20cm. (Photo: So-Nouveau)

2.119 Hutton pewter lidded jug with blue Ruskin cabochons, c.1905, h. 17 cm. (Photo: Tony Victoria Gallery New York)

2.120 Hutton pewter lidded jug with a heart-shaped blue Ruskin cabochon on the top, 1905, h. 15.5 cm. (Photo: FCR Gallery London)

2.121 Hutton lidded jug with blue stone and maiden handle (model 0616) designed by Kate Harris 1904, h. 31 cm. (Photo: FCR Gallery London)

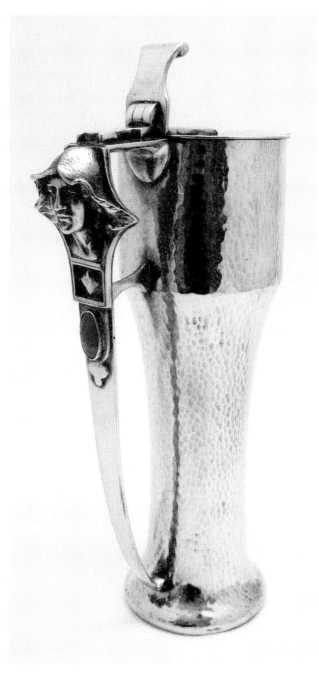

Detail of the lidded jug in Plate 2.121. (Photo: FCR Gallery London)

2.122 Cornish Arts & Crafts repousse pewter charger with fish motif designed by Elsie Morgan c.1905, d. 40 cm. (Photo courtesy Linda Sutton)

2.123 Cornish Arts & Crafts repousse pewter charger with fish motif designed by Elsie Morgan c.1905, d. 40 cm. (Photo courtesy Linda Sutton)

COPPER AND PEWTER WORK   DESIGNED BY H. J. MARYON.   EXECUTED
BY T. SPARKS, J. RICHARDSON,
T. CLARK AND R. TEMPLE

2.124 A group of Keswick School of Industrial Arts pewter and copperware designed by H.J. Maryon. (Photo: *The Studio* c.1902)

2.125 Wrought Pewter inlaid green stained oak sideboard designed by M.H. Baillie Scott 1904. (Photo *The Studio* 1904)

2.126 Hugh Wallis pewter inlayed copper bowl c.1925, d. 20 cm.
(Woolley & Wallis)

2.127 Left and centre: Pewter mounted Ruskin brooches by Guild Button Company, c.1910. (FCR Gallery London) Right: Pewter mounted Ruskin brooch by Plantagenet, c.1910. (FCR Gallery London)

2.128 Pewter glass lined salt by Homeland pewter of Sheffield c.1910, h. 3 cm. (Photo: FCR Gallery London)

2.129 Homeland pewter cake basket/fruit bowl with basket weave handle. This was very much in the Liberty house style, c.1920, h. 23 cm. (Photo: Clare Weatherall)

2.130 English Pewter tea set designed by Harold Stabler for James Dixon & Sons c.1928, h. 19 cm. (Photo: Cromwells Antiques Centre Hertfordshire)

2.131 Pewter coffee pot with ebony handle and finial designed by Harold Stabler for James Dixons & Sons c.1928, h. 19 cm. (Photo: FCR Gallery London)

2.132 Charles Boyton pewter coffee pot for James Dixon & Sons with walnut handle and finial, 1935, h. 19 cm. (Private Collection London)

2.133 Charles Boyton pewter sugar bowl for James Dixon & Sons with walnut finial, 1935, w. 16 cm. (Private Collection London)

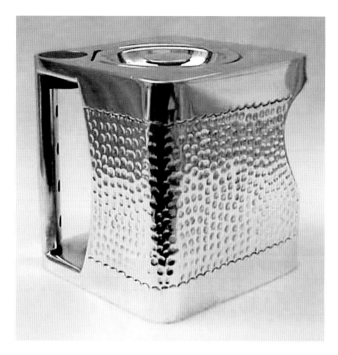

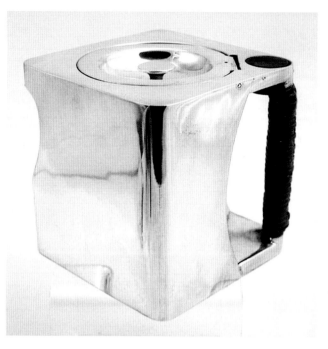

2.134 Cube teapot with planished pewter finish designed by Robert Crawford Johnson for T.W&S c.1917, h. 10 cm. This teapot was used in the first class section of the *Queen Mary* ocean liner. (Photo: FCR Gallery London)

2.135 Cube teapot designed by Robert Crawford Johnson for T.W&S c.1917, h. 10 cm. This teapot was used in the first class section of the *Queen Mary* ocean liner. (Photo: FCR Gallery London)

2.136 English Art Nouveau Pewter bowl with kneeling maidens, c.1910, marked L&B English Pewter. This is believed to have been manufactured in Sheffield. d. 28 cm. (Photo: Ian Aldridge)

2.137 English Arts & Crafts planished pewter and Ruskin mirror c.1910, 23 x 41 cm. (FCR Gallery London)

2.138 Pewter Ruskin photo frame with tulip motif. This is typical of items produced in night schools around the UK c.1900-1920, 18 x 30 cm. (Photo FCR Gallery London)

2.139 Scottish School repousse block tin mirror with floral motif c.1910, 57 x 29cm. (Lyon & Turnbull)

2.140 Scottish School repousse block tin mirror with Celtic knot-work set with turquoise Ruskin roundels c.1910, 72 x 41cm. (Lyon & Turnbull)

2.141 Scottish School repousse white metal mirror with enamel inserts framed in fruitwood c.1900, 36 x 50cm. (FCR Gallery London)

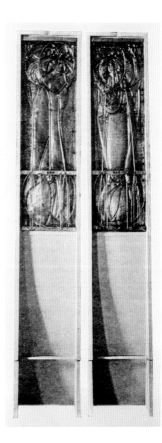

2.142 Beaten lead pewter fire surround designed by C.R. Mackintosh for the White Room at Miss Cranston's Ingram Street Tea Rooms c.1903. (Photo: *The Studio* 1903)

2.143 A pair of pewter repousse panels designed by Herbert and Frances McNair exhibited in the Scottish room of the Turin Exhibition 1902. (Photo: *The Studio* 1903, vol 28)

2.144 Charles Rennie Mackintosh pewter and abalone shell inset mahogany mirror for Ingram Street Tea Rooms, Glasgow c.1900. (James Strang, Glasgow)

Detail of Plate 2.144.

2.145 English Arts and Crafts repousse pewter screen with glass cabochons c.1900, 90 cm x 40 cm. (Nicole Tinero)

2.146 Talwin Morris repousse admiralty brass panel for Morris' office at Blackie's Design in Glasgow c.1900. (James Strang, Glasgow)

2.147 Margaret Gilmour repousse block tin pewter picture frame with inset mother of pearl roundel c.1900. (James Strang, Glasgow)

2.148 Alexander Ritchie repousse pewter mirror with Celtic entrelac decoration c.1910. (James Strang, Glasgow)

Examples of Makers' Marks

3.1 A pewter figural Art Nouveau *Cueillette des iris* vase by Auguste Moreau
c.1900, h. 43.5cm. (The Dorotheum, Vienna)

FRENCH PEWTER

In the late nineteenth century France was indisputably the artistic hub of the world. It attracted new and vibrant talent from all corners of the globe. The Belle Époque captured the public's imagination and influenced all forms of fine and applied arts.

There is no doubt that Britain had an influence on the development of the Art Nouveau style in France. The Arts & Crafts movement in England was at its pinnacle at this point in history. The second-generation pre-Raphaelite painters were involved with William Morris, designing and exhibiting new and exciting decorative arts at the various guilds and societies around Britain. A similar prevalence of exhibitions also took place in Paris. The most important being the annual Salon exhibitions of French fine and applied arts. These lavishly mounted competitions attracted up to 23,000 people daily, ranking them amongst the most popular leisure attractions of their time. Paris also mounted the Exposition Universelle in 1900, placing it in the forefront to promote French design to an international market.

The term Art Nouveau was derived from the name of the Paris gallery, L'Art Nouveau. It was founded by Siegfried (Samuel) Bing 1838-1905 (Plate 0.4). Bing exhibited at the Exposition Universelle in 1900 as 'Art Nouveau Bing' and received favourable reviews for his discerning eye. Bing was an admirer of the British Aesthetic and Arts & Crafts movements, making regular trips to Britain. He began importing objects, prints and textiles from Japan and, much like William Morris and Arthur Liberty, saw the commercial potential in championing a western adaptation of this exotic style. Bing also retailed objects made by many of the top British, German and American designers of the period.

Between 1898-1905 there were as many as 200 sculptors working in *étain* (French pewter). Many of these artists were already known for their high quality bronze pieces. Foundries also produced objects in spelter, a material similar to pewter but with a higher zinc content. Spelter was brittle and the objects were quite fragile as a result. A strong, inexpensive alternative to bronze was needed and pewter coated with a variety of applied faux bronze and gilt patination was the logical solution.

Art Nouveau is noted for its use of whiplash design elements. Contemporary critics often endearingly referred to this as 'spaghetti-like' in form. This key design component made its debut in French pewter in the late nineteenth century. The sculptor Auguste Moreau[1] produced a number of fine designs in both the Art Nouveau and Neo Classical styles. Many of the designs, including lamps and centrepieces, depicted heraldic women with entwining whiplash floral motifs (see opposite). Another artist working in this style was Julien Causse (b. 1869). Honoured at the Paris Exhibition in 1900, he produced a number of items portraying naturalistic images of sensual women (Plate 3.17). Fine examples of Art Nouveau pewter were produced to satisfy the demand for this new and exciting style, the most refined pieces being those designed by Jules Paul Brateau.

Jules Paul Brateau (1844-1923) won a gold medal at the 1889 Paris Exhibition for his Neo Classical ewer and bowl depicting 'The Sciences and The Arts'.[2] Both pieces were hand-carved in reverse, utilising plaster and then cast (Plates 3.2, 3.3 and 3.4). The process was labour-intensive and time-consuming. It is suggested that it took over two years to produce this one commission.[3]

There is no doubt that Brateau spearheaded the revival of pewter in France. He was one of the first artists whose concern was not hindered by the intrinsic value of the material, but by the purity of the object itself. The magnificent table clock created in 1901 in the Symbolist style and fashioned in pewter with a blue enamel face

1. Auguste Louis M. Moreau (1834-1917): French sculptor known for his heraldic and Art Nouveau bronzes exhibited at the Société des Artistes Français in 1900. Many models were also cast in spelter or pewter.
2. Jules Brateau (1844-1923): sculptor, jeweller and pewtersmith, known as the person who revived the art of pewter casting in France. He won a gold medal at the Exposition Universelle of 1889, for his 'The Arts & Sciences' ewer and charger made in relief pewter casting.
3. Boucaud, Jean-Christophe, *Jules Brateau: 1844-1923*, Mavaussan (Herault), 2003.

exemplifies this aesthetic. Traditionally a clock of this sophistication would be produced in silver. However Brateau chose to work in pewter due to its malleability and soft lustre (Plate 3.2).

Many of the artists working in pewter were respected sculptors, a further affirmation of the crossover occurring between fine and applied arts in both subject and form. The Art Nouveau maiden was an extremely popular motif in French pewter several of the designs are depicted in the avant-garde Symbolist style with minimal facial features set in romantic and exotic land and seascapes.

Jules Desbois (1851-1935) was another well-established French sculptor working in bronze and marble. He worked in the studio/workshop of the sculptor Rodin and is noted for his fine original work in pewter (Plates 3.13 and 3.14).

It is difficult to speculate which country can be credited for popularising the sensuous depiction of the female form in commercial Art Nouveau pewter design. The Germans were very good at adapting international styles. However, it seems that the French were a few years ahead in this area. Many of the early German designs seem to derive from French bronze virtue from this period (See Plates 1.46 and 1.51).

Another notable sculptor working in pewter was **Maurice Bouval** (Plate 3.25). His pewter and gilt bronze jardinière naturalistically depicts a sinuous floral design with a contrasting female figure in gilt bronze.

In Paris pewter was retailed through the Grande Magazins Printemps and Galerie Lafayette, as well as specialist home furnishing boutiques and smaller jewellery shops. The mass retailing of pewter objects was not limited to the capital and spread throughout provincial France. Nancy was also a popular centre for the Art Nouveau movement and pewter proved a popular medium.

Another respected French firm to use pewter was **Christofle**. Founded in 1830 by Charles Christofle, the firm purchased the patent for silver electroplating from the British manufacturer Elkington in 1842. At the turn of the twentieth century they marketed a range of Art Nouveau inspired objects under the name Gallia and commissioned well known designers, such as Felix Cheron, to execute designs in pewter (Plate 3.5).

The well respected designers **Abel Landry** and **Maurice Dufrene** also worked in pewter some were commissioned for the Maison Moderne, an exclusive Paris emporium.

W. Hareng designed vases and jardinières in an opulent Art Nouveau style (Plate 3.8). These larger items were often decorated with maiden, floral and nautical motifs.

Etain Garranti was another French factory known for their quirky designs, many of which were by the artist J. Garnier. Grotesque birds and sinuous maidens and dolphins climbing the sides of jugs and vases were typical subjects for this factory. It is thought that some of the designs were inspired by the English pottery, Martin Bros. of Southall.

Claude Bonnefond was a sculptor known for his work in pewter. He designed many decorative items including candlesticks, clocks, lamps and trays for the firm Susses Freres Paris, signing his pieces C. Bonnefond. They were retailed internationally.

French Art Nouveau pewter is known for its unabashed, flamboyant style. It continues to be highly regarded by collectors of early twentieth century metalware today. Many of the major foundries and firms closed at the start of the First World War, however pewter re-emerged as a fashionable medium during the Art Deco period, especially in its use in modernist lamps and dinanderie.

The jeweller and designer **Jean Després** is regarded as a leading light in the production of pewter in the Art Deco period. Després produced a variety of objects in étain ranging from vases to bowls and presentation trophies. Profoundly influenced by Cubism and Futurism, Després developed a unique approach to design, which is now categorised as Machine Age Modern. His use of cogs, wheels and other machine-like components give his work a dynamism which is closer in character to Modernist sculpture than much of the design of the period.

Eugène Chanal (1872-1925) and **Alice Chanal** (1872-1951) were a husband and wife team who created a range of Modernist pewter in the 1920s and 1930s. They were often patinated to look like bronze or gilded in a mellow gold finish. Their forms were bold and organic utilising enlarged floral motifs (Plates 3.29 and 3.30).

3.2 French pewter clock with enamelled dial by Jules Paul Brateau c.1901, h. 35 cm. This clock was exhibited at the Salon de la Societe National des Beaux-Arts. The side of the clock reveals the motto '*Hora. Sit. Optima. Cvnctis*' ('Let Us Count The Happy Hours In Full'). The clock is believed to depict Adam and Eve with Atlas holding up the world at the top standing on palm leaves, mistletoe and wings. The base is a sunflower, which is reaching for the sun on the dial. (Photo: Virginia Museum of Fine Arts, Richmond, USA)

3.4 Brateau pewter goblet with leaves and inscription c.1905, h. 15cm. (Photo: Philippe CHAPEAU)

3.3 Brateau pewter goblet with raspberries and inscription c.1905, h. 11.5cm. (Photo: Philippe CHAPEAU)

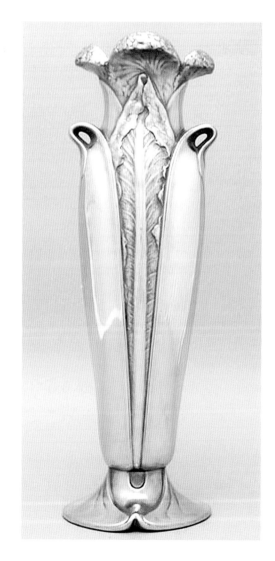

3.5 Pair of French pewter candlesticks designed by Felix Cheron for Gallia (Christofle) exhibited 1902, h. 30cm. (FCR Gallery London)

3.6 A Christofle Gallia pewter vase with floral decoration motif c.1900, h. 36cm. (Titus Omega)

3.7 French pewter wine coaster designed by Felix Cheron for Gallia (Christofle) exhibited 1902, d. 12cm. (FCR Gallery London)

3.8 (Right) French Pewter jardinière designed by W. Hareng depicting two boys catching a Siren in their fishing net with a mermaid coming from behind to slap them, c.1902, h. 33cm. It is possible that W. Hareng was in fact a pseudonym for Elsie Ward Hering an American sculptor living in Paris c.1900. See: *Etains*, Philippe Dahhan, Les Editions de L'Amateur, 2000. (FCR Gallery London)

3.9 A pair of Christofle Gallia pewter spill vases with stag beetle motif (model 4842) c.1900, h. 17.5cm. (Woolley & Wallis)

3.10 A Gallia Art Nouveau pewter jug (model 4341) made by Christofle c.1903, h. 24cm. (Private collection London)

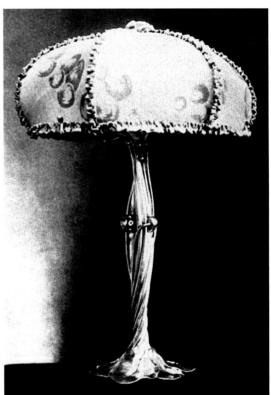

3.11 French Pewter lamp designed by Abel Landry for La Maison Moderne, Paris, c.1902-1904.

3.12 Alfred-Louis-Archille Daguet glove box. Wood covered in repousse pewter, copper and brass c.1910, l. 33cm, h. 10.3cm, w. 10cm.
(Private collection London)

3.13 Jules Desbois Symbolist pewter plate 'Eve' c.1900, d. 24cm.
(Photo: Philippe Chapeau)

3.14 Jules Desbois Symbolist pewter plate 'Hebe', c.1900, d. 24cm.
(Photo: Private collection Boston)

3.15 French pewter casket in the style of Hector Guimard c.1900, w. 18cm. (FCR Gallery London)

3.16 A French pewter two-branch candelabra in the style of Victor Horta c.1900, h. 30cm. (Liz & Les Hall-Bakker)

3.17 Art Nouveau bronze patinated pewter figure lamp by J. Causse, c.1900, model 'Lys', h. 52cm. (Twentieth Century Decorative Arts UK)

3.18 pewter and ceramic inkwell most likely designed by Jean Garnier c.1905 in the style of the English ceramic firm Martin Bros. This inkwell has often been attributed to the firm Reinemann en Lichtinger, a German company known for their production of beer steins. Unmarked, h. 10cm. (FCR Gallery London)

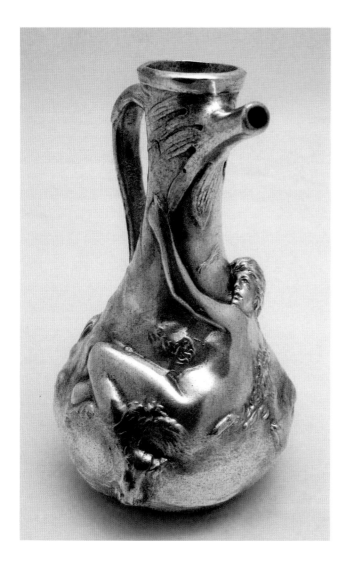

3.19 A French pewter jug depicting a water nymph swimming with dolphins by Jean Garnier c.1902, h. 18cm. (FCR Gallery London)

3.20 A French pewter jug depicting a baby bird by Jean Garnier c.1902, h. 16.5cm. There are other examples of this jug that have been signed 'Petiz', the signature of Emile Petizon. (FCR Gallery London)

3.21 A French pewter cedar-lined cigarette box depicting a woman smoking c.1900, w. 15cm. (FCR Gallery London)

3.22 A pair of French Art Nouveau candlesticks in the style of Juventa c.1900, h. 17cm. (Sandy Stanley)

3.23 Pewter clock designed by Bonnefond c.1900. This Art Nouveau inspired clock was popular and many examples were produced, h. 30cm. (Quinty's Art Nouveau)

3.24 Bonnefond candelabrum. These were perhaps the best known of the Bonnefond designs. c.1900, h. 36cm. (Photo: Sjöström Antik Stockholm)

3.25 Pewter and gilt bronze jardinière 'Nue Assise' by Maurice Bouval c.1900, h. 18cm, w. 34cm. (Photo Dan Root/Macklowe Gallery NYC)

3.26 A pair of French gilt pewter candelabra with Adam and Eve figures depicted in the Art Nouveau style, c.1900, h. 28cm, unmarked. (FCR Gallery London)

3.28 Jean Després Modernist vase in hammered pewter c.1930, h. 14cm.
(Photo: Galerie Vallois)

3.27 A French Art Nouveau spill vase c.1900,
h. 15cm. (So-Nouveau)

3.29 Art Deco gilt pewter vase
designed by Parisians Alice and
Eugene Chanal c.1920, h. 35cm.
(Van Den Akker Antiques)

3.30 Organic Art Deco
pewter vase designed by
Alice and Eugene Chanal
c.1920, h. 34.5cm.
(FCR Gallery London)

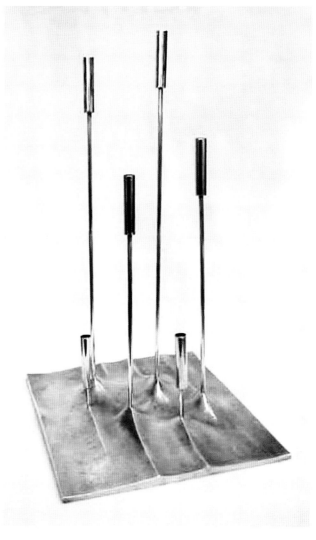

3.31 French Modernist pewter head in the style of Brancusi unsigned c.1930, h. 16cm. (FCR Gallery London)

3.32 Christofle Gallia 'Sol Lumiere' mid-century Modernist candleholder designed by Tapio Wirkkala with six inset holders of graduating heights, the tallest 31cm. (FCR Gallery London)

Examples of Makers' Marks

DUTCH PEWTER

The Netherlands contribution to the international Art Nouveau movement was aptly named Nieuwe Kunst ('New Art'). They excelled in areas of furniture design, ceramics and metalwork. The region produced at least one outstanding pewter firm, notably Urania. This important company manufactured pewterware of the highest quality with innovative and expressive decoration.

The **Urania** factory (founded in 1903) was located in Maastricht on the border of Germany. It created a wide range of distinctive objects for the German taste. Urania set up retail outlets in Berlin and Aken. The company exhibited at international fairs and their goods were widely exported. The German designer Friedrich Adler was invited to submit production designs and a number of superb examples of his work were manufactured, many with his trademark spine decoration.

Juventa Prima Metal was another distinguished name, producing a selection of fine pewter objects. Until recently, it was thought that Juventa was a Dutch firm. However, it has been suggested that the designer Hans Peter (of WMF) was behind the creation of this brand and that the output was produced by his factory across the border in Esslingen, Germany.[1]

The quality of Juventa pewter is unsurpassed. Many items have a sinuous whiplash decoration and at least one model has Loetz Papillon glass mounted in an organic floral pewter frame. The origin of the Juventa factory is still not identified. However, two examples of an identical vase have been found, one bearing the 'Juventa' mark and another signed 'HP' and 'Royal-zinn'; this further suggests that this line of pewter was created by Hans Peter (Plate 1.219).

The English Connection

Both Urania and Juventa were imported into the UK in the early part of the twentieth century. It is acknowledged that Hutton of Sheffield bought some of the moulds from the Urania factory.[2] They continued production of these models in the UK and retailed them through Connell of Cheapside (London). These items are usually marked Urania Hutton Sheffield or Urania Connell of Cheapside. The quantity of items available in the UK leads me to believe that both ranges were retailed through Liberty & Co.

Modernism in Holland

A period of growth and prosperity after the First World War led to the birth of *De Stijl* ('The Style'), an artistic movement founded in 1917 by Theo van Doesburg a painter, writer and designer. The group also included Gerrit Rietveld and the important abstract painter Piet Mondrian. The term *De Stijl* refers to a body of work from 1917 to 1931, which utilised clean, simple lines and primary colours to express ultimate simplicity and abstraction. The straight line and rectangle became the basis of Rietveld's design ethos. It is reflected in the later work of the designer Cris Agterberg's cubist tea set designed in 1930 (Plate 4.13).

1. Graham Dry Juventa, *Sammlerjournal* 28, 1999.
2. Urania Maastricht 1903-1910 Jan C. G. Kwint p.23.

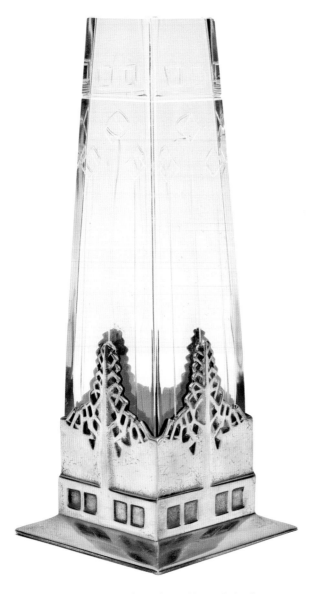

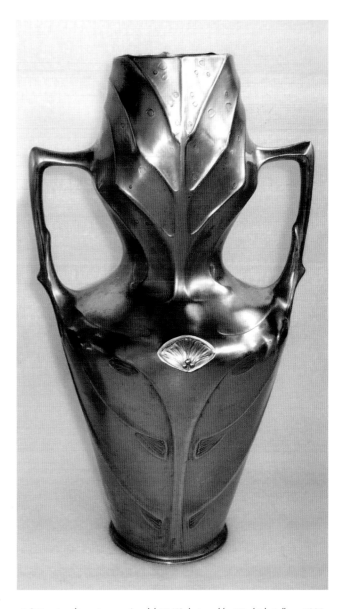

4.1 Urania pewter and crystal vase designed by Friedrich Adler c.1901, h. 30cm. (Sergei Glebov)

4.2 Urania gilt pewter vase (model 1140) designed by Friedrich Adler c.1905, h. 36cm. (Quinty's Art Nouveau)

4.3 Urania pewter basket (model 1113) c.1904, h. 26cm. (FCR Gallery London)

4.5 Urania pewter fruit bowl (model 1145) designed by Friedrich Adler c.1903, d. 27cm. (FCR Gallery London)

4.4 Urania pewter-mounted glass vase c.1903, h. 28cm. (Quinty's Art Nouveau)

4.6 Urania pewter candlestick c.1905, h. 15cm. (FCR Gallery London)

4.7 Urania pewter basket (model 1112) c.1904, l. cm. (FCR Gallery London)

4.8 Urania pewter and oak tray (model 1005) 52 x 30cm.
(FCR Gallery London)

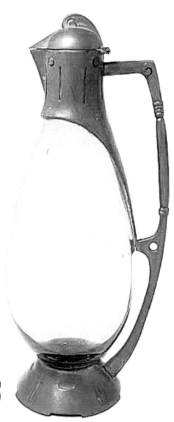

4.9 Urania pewter-mounted green glass jug
c.1905, h. 23cm. (FCR Gallery London)

4.10 Urania pewter bowl with rose hip decoration c.1904, d. 17cm.
(DC London)

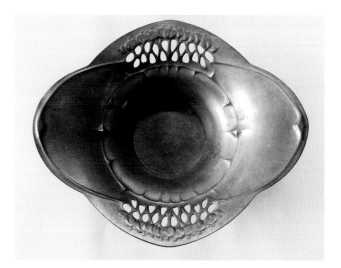

4.11 Urania pewter cake dish with handle and floral design 1904, l. 22cm.
(Photo: DC London)

4.12 Urania pewter ice bucket/jardinière (model 1008) designed by Friedrich
Adler c.1905, h.17cm. (FCR Gallery London)

4.13 Dutch Modernist pewter and rosewood 6-piece tea set and tray designed by Cris Agterberg c.1930. (The Centraal Museum Utrecht)

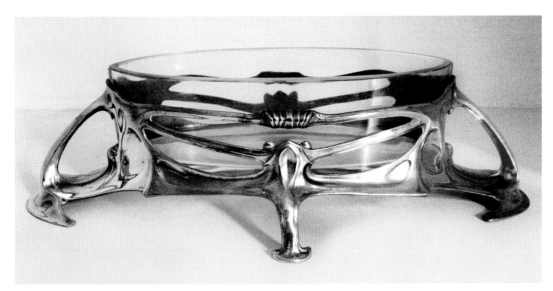

4.14 Urania pewter and crystal centrepiece designed by Friedrich Adler (model 1011) c.1904, l. 34cm. (FCR Gallery London)

4.15 Dutch Modernist pewter and Bakelite sugar bowl designed by Theodore Hooft (1918-1965) for Gero, Zeist, Holland, c.1930, h. 11.7cm. (FCR Gallery London)

Examples of Makers' Marks

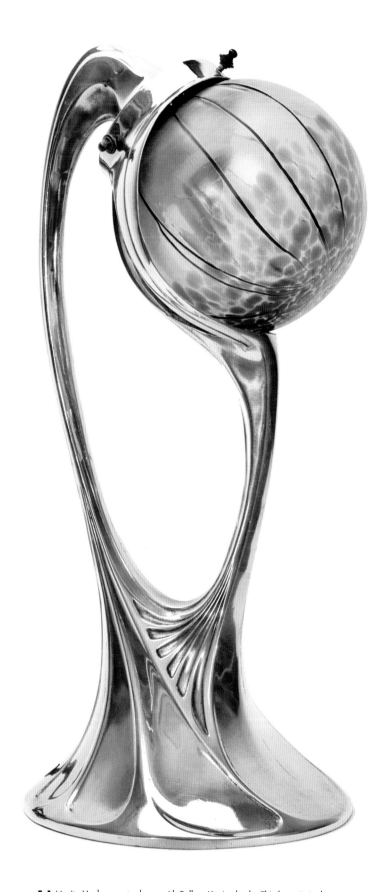

5.1 Moritz Hacker pewter lamp with Pallme Konig shade. This lamp is in the Gustav Gurschner style and may very well have been designed by him c.1905, h. 42 cm. (Collection Sergei Glebov)

AUSTRIAN PEWTER

In 1900 Vienna had a thriving artistic community of painters, architects and designers. Many of the leading exponents were involved in the Vereiningung Bildender Künstler Österreichs (Union of Austrian Artists), which amalgamated to form the Vienna Secession Movement.[1] Joseph Maria Olbrich was commissioned to design an opulent purpose built exhibition space for annual events and Gustav Klimt[2] was elected as the first president of the group (Plate 5.2).

The Wiener Werkstätte was a radical modernist collective whose directive was to redesign the twentieth century, notably its architecture, interiors and fashion. Founded by Josef Hoffmann and Koloman Moser,[3] both professors at the Kunstgewer-Beschule (School of Applied Arts), the Wiener Werkstätte had a profound influence on international design of the period. There are several examples of twentieth-century pewter which incorporated elements of Hoffmann and Moser silver designs into their creations. WMF was especially fond of the cut-out and embossed square decoration, a hallmark of the Wiener Werkstätte. Many of their designers were inspired by the Secession Movement, which was a clear breakaway from the over-decorated Art Nouveau style (Plate 5.4).

Argentor (C. A. Münchmeyer & Co.)

The name Argentor is a compound word formed by joining the French words for silver (*argent*) and gold (*or*). C. A. Münchmeyer & Co. was founded by Carl Adalbert Münchmeyer and Ferdinand Ernst Rust in 1863. The company quickly acquired a superior reputation for the production of fine silver, silver-plate and pewterware establishing workshops in Berlin and Vienna. In 1894, Adolf Wilhelm Hetzel joined the Vienna factory and under the guidance of Ernst Rust, he rebranded the company Argentor in 1902.

Argentor produced a high quality range of pewter in both the Art Nouveau and Secessionist styles. By 1912 the company had thousands of items in production

making it one of the largest companies after WMF.

It is quite possible that Koloman Moser designed some of the pewter mounts for Loetz glass although there is no record of him designing for the firm. It is known that Hans Ofner a minor member of the Wiener Werkstätte and a student of Josef Hoffman designed a number of the Secessionist models for the Argentor factory (Plate 5.3).

A.K. & Cie

Founded in Vienna in the 1880s by Albert Kohler, A.K. & Cie produced high quality silverware, silver plate, and bronze castings. The company commissioned designs by the German Darmstadt architect Peter Behrens including a pewter mirror which was exhibited in the Austrian pavilion at the 1902 Turin Exhibition (Plate 5.5).

A.K.& Cie was bought by WMF in 1900 and continued to produce some of its original output, but also many of the known WMF models. The merger opened up WMF to the lucrative Austrian Hungarian market and they continued to export items there until 1914.

Moritz Hacker

Moritz Hacker, or to use their full trading name 'k. & k. Hof-Silber-und Chinasilberwarenfabrik Moritz Hacker', were best known for their exceptional pewter in the Vienna Secessionist style. This outstanding Austrian company exported wares all over Europe and North America. They also worked in the popular Art Nouveau style producing accessories such as inkwells, cigarette boxes, centrepieces and clocks. In 1898 they opened an office in Budapest, thereby expanding into the thriving Hungarian market. Moritz Hacker created pewter mounts of note for Loetz glass in the Secessionist style of Josef Hoffmann and Koloman Moser utilising mounts with square and round cut-outs. The company showed their products at the Exhibition of Austrian Arts & Crafts in Vienna in 1901.[4]

---

1. The Secessionist Movement or the Vienna Secession (1897-1939) was a group of artists led by Gustav Klimt and included the painters, designers and architects Josef Hoffmann, Koloman Moser, Otto Wagner and J. M. Olbrich.
2. Gustav Klimt was an Austrian painter (1862-1918) working in the Art Nouveau style using a rich bright palette and often gold leaf. He was influenced by the Byzantine mosaics of Ravenna.

3. The architect Josef Hoffmann (1870-1956) and painter and designer Koloman Moser (1868-1918), both from Austria, developed a style together which was at the forefront of the Modernist movement.
4. W. Neuwirth, *Blühender Jugendstil*, vol. II, Vienna 1991

5.2 Detail of the Secession building in Vienna designed by J.M. Olbrich c.1899.

5.3 Argentor silver-plated Britannia metal-mounted crystal bowl (model 4123) designed by Hans Ofner c.1904 h. 23 cm. (FCR Gallery London)

5.4 An Austrian pewter and brass architectural inkstand in the style of Josef Hoffmann made by A.K. & Cie. This inkstand shows the influence of the Wiener Werkstätte with its embossed and cut out squares, c.1905, w. 34 cm. (FCR Gallery London)

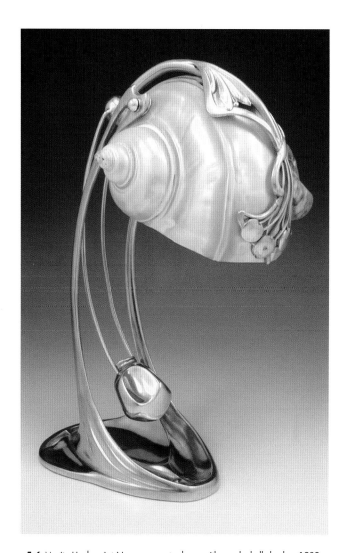

5.5 A.K. & Cie pewter table mirror designed by Peter Behrens c.1900, h. 42 cm. (FCR Gallery London)

5.6 Moritz Hacker Art Nouveau pewter lamp with conch shell shade c.1902, h. 40cm. (Titus Omega)

5.7 A.K. & Cie pewter and wood wine service designed by Peter Behrens c.1900, w. 39 cm. (FCR Gallery London)

5.8 Argentor pewter and nautilus shell lamp c.1905, h. 68 cm. (Titus Omega)

5.9 Argentor pewter lamp c.1905, h. 77cm. (Titus Omega)

5.10 Argentor pewter sweetmeats tray with Art Nouveau maiden c.1905, h. 22 cm. (Titus Omega)

5.11 Argentor pewter twin branch candelabra (models 3330/3331c) 1905, h. 35 cm. (Titus Omega)

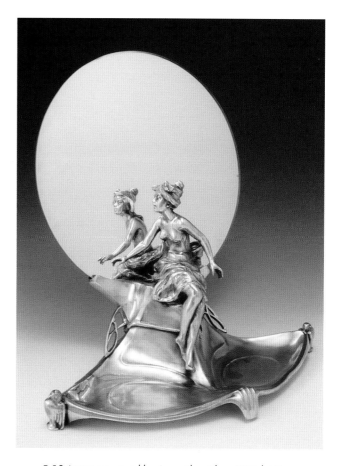

5.12 Argentor pewter table mirror with floral decoration c.1905, h. 40cm. (So-Nouveau)

5.13 Argentor pewter table mirror with maiden c.1905, h. 70cm. (Titus Omega)

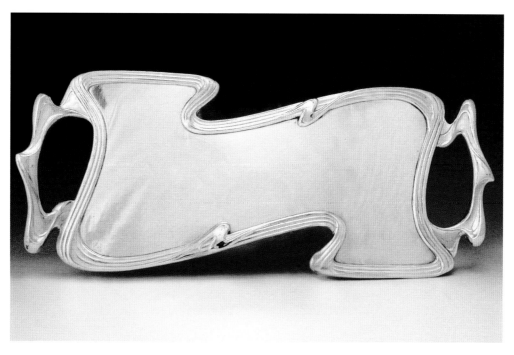

5.14 Argentor pewter tray in an organic Art Nouveau style reminiscent of Henri Van de Velde (model 3914) c.1900, w. 50 cm. (Titus Omega)

5.15 Argentor a pair of Gilt pewter Vienna Jugendstil jardinières
(model 3740) executed by Argentor, Vienna c.1900, l. 24.5 cm,
h. 12 cm. (Photo Bel Etage)

5.17 Argentor pewter clock with sunrise motif (model 4888) c.1905, h.30 cm.
(FCR Gallery London)

5.16 Argentor pewter and Loetz Pampas pattern glass vase c.1900,
h.23 cm. (Robert Petersen Decorative Arts)

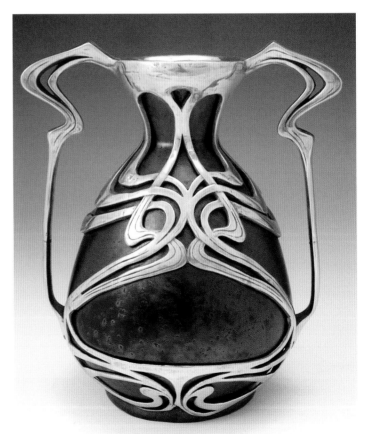

5.18 Moritz Hacker pewter-mounted Loetz Phanomen glass vase
c.1902 h. 24 cm. (Titus Omega)

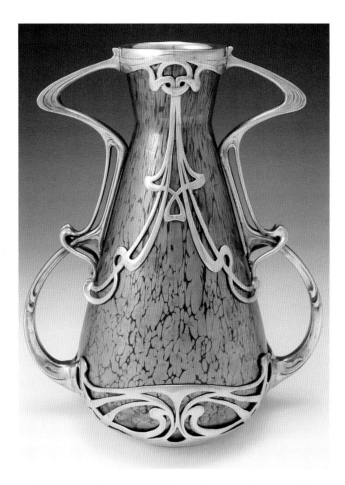

5.19 Moritz Hacker pewter-mounted Loetz Phanomen glass vase c.1905, h. 26 cm. (Titus Omega)

5.20 Moritz Hacker pewter-mounted Loetz Papillon glass vase c.1902, h. 26 cm. (Titus Omega)

5.22 Argentor pewter-mounted Loetz glass vase c.1902, h. 24 cm. (FCR Gallery London)

5.21 Argentor pewter-mounted Loetz glass vase (model 4367) c.1902, h. 24 cm. (Titus Omega)

5.23 Moritz Hacker pewter Art Nouveau tea caddy c.1905, w. 13cm. (Titus Omega)

5.25 Moritz Hacker pewter and brass Art Nouveau centrepiece c.1905, w. 55cm. (Titus Omega)

5.24 Moritz Hacker gilt pewter-mounted iridescent glass vase c.1902, h.24 cm. (FCR Gallery London)

5.26 Pewter figural Art Nouveau clock by Argentor c.1904, h. 38cm. (Titus Omega)

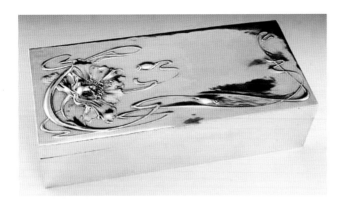

5.27 Moritz Hacker pewter cedar-lined cigar box c.1905, w. 27cm.
(Titus Omega)

5.28 Karl Hagenauer repousse tin box with integral glass liner c.1920,
l. 25cm, w. 14cm, h. 8.5cm. Base stamped 'wHw' and 'MADE IN AUSTRIA'.
(Private Collection London)

5.29 K. & K. Hof-Silber-und Chinasilberwarenfabrik Moritz Hacker pewter
centrepiece with crystal liner and blue glass columns in the Vienna Secessionist
style, 1910, h. 31.4cm, w. 32.5cm, d. 22cm. (Photo Bel Etage)

5.30 J. & J. Herrmann, Vienna, mahogany cabinet with geometric inlay in
pewter, white metal fittings and faceted cut glass decorated with rose
ornaments, 1905, h. 180cm, w. 90cm, d. 45cm. (Photo: Bel Etage)

5.31 An Austrian Secessionist mahogany club chair inlayed with pewter,
ebony and mother of pearl c.1905. (FCR Gallery London)

5.32 K. & K. Hof-Silber-und Chinasilberwarenfabrik Moritz Hacker pewter
mantel clock with blue glass columns in the Vienna Secessionist style, 1910,
h. 35cm, w. 29.5cm, d. 17cm. (Photo Bel Etage)

Examples of Makers' Marks

SCANDINAVIAN PEWTER

In the first quarter of the twentieth century, Scandinavia embarked on a renaissance of decorative arts that would continue to dominate design into the twenty-first century. Sweden and Denmark produced important examples of Arts & Crafts metalware, glass and ceramics. Norway also created notable items in pewter and silver, some with enamel.

Mogens Ballin

The Danish firm of Mogens Ballin were among the first to make the transition into the 'youth style' (*Jugendstil*). The workshop was set up in 1900 with the help of the sculptor Siegfried Wagner. They produced a number of unusual bowls, lamps and vases in pewter, brass and copper. They also made an extraordinary range of silver jewellery.

In 1901 Mogens Ballin hired sculptor Georg Jensen (1866-1935) who stayed with the firm for a number of years, designing and producing a range of items in silver. German and French styles may have inspired Mogens Ballin. However, the overall sentiment remains uniquely Danish in its approach to decoration. Naturalistic motifs (Plate 6.1) were inspired by French designs of the period, but had a simplified austerity that is purely Scandinavian. Georg Jensen remained with Mogens Ballin until 1904 when he set up his own workshop. Jensen exhibited internationally and soon his reputation achieved a global status. This success inspired other small firms to market products outside of Denmark.

Just Andersen

Just Andersen (1844-1943) was a designer based in Copenhagen who exported his goods internationally. He originally created objects in the Art Nouveau style, but soon moved into a far more successful range of early Art Deco and Modernist designs in pewter, bronze and copper (Plates 6.31-6.41). Andersen notably formulated an original pewter alloy which he called Disko metal. It was made up of tin, lead and antimony, which was then patinated with various realistic bronze finishes.

Other notable Danish designers were Aegte Ildfast, Hans Kongele and Knud Anderson, although their preferred medium was bronze.

Sweden's close proximity to Germany made it a key market for imports of decorative arts from this region. WMF and Kayserzinn pewter were retailed in the larger city centres and this inspired a wave of domestic pewter production.

Schreuder & Olsson

The most original and sought after makers of Swedish Art Nouveau pewter were Schreuder & Olsson of Stockholm. They designed a line of pewter items including candlesticks, lamps, vases and inkstands, usually incorporating swirling water with fish (Plates 6.4-6.9). These are reminiscent of Hugo Leven's designs for Kayserzinn and some of Walter Scherf's Osiris production, but with a definite Scandinavian flair.

A number of Swedish items including a candelabrum in the style of the French designer Bonnefond were popular. Many of these designs can be found at auction and at antiques fairs today confirming the extent to which Sweden grasped the Art Nouveau style. Examples of unmarked WMF-type calling card trays and tazzas, some exactly replicating the original models, are also common. It is quite possible that WMF had an association with one of the Swedish retailers or perhaps designs were bought in or licensed by a Swedish firm.

In the years between the wars, Sweden became a hotbed of talent in the area of industrial design. As with Bing & Co. in Paris at the turn of the twentieth century, Sweden's artistic energy needed an uncompromising venue to showcase its exceptional items. The result was the department store named Svenskt Tenn.

Svenskt Tenn

Svenskt Tenn (Swedish Pewter) was formed with the vision to explore and promote these avant-garde tastes. Founded in 1924 by designer Estrid Ericson (1894-1981) and Nils Fougstedt (1881-1954), Svenskt Tenn was not just a shop selling pewter, but an interior/lifestyle firm, which set the precedent for much of the important design to emerge from Sweden throughout the twentieth century. The shop opened its doors in 1924 and is still fashionable today.

6.1 Mogens Ballin Danish Art Nouveau pewter bowl with dragonfly motif.
c.1902 d. 23cm. (Didier Antiques London)

Svenskt Tenn hired talented, innovative designers, including the Wiener Werkstätte architect Josef Frank. Other notable names identified with this firm were, Edvin Ohrstrom, Anna Petrus and Uno Åhrén. Out of all of the designers at Svenskt Tenn, Nils Fougstedt emerged as one of the leading pewter designers of his day with his futuristic inspired vases and bowls (Plates 6.24 and 6.25).

Hallberg

The achievement of Svenskt Tenn prompted many other firms in Sweden to begin pewter production. Guldsmedsaktiebolaget (G.A.B.) and Hallberg, well-established silversmiths, produced ranges of modernist pewter in the 1920's and 1930's.

Hallberg hired the designer Sylvia Stave to create a range of interesting objects including vases, cocktail shakers and jugs. In many ways they were reminiscent of pieces by Fougstedt (Plates 6.29 and 6.30), but they also derived inspiration from England's Christopher Dresser and the German Bauhaus designers Christian Dell and Marianne Brandt.

G.A.B.

G.A.B. also had a successful range of pewter. Some of it was designed by the innovative Folke Arstrom (1907-1997) who used streamlining and modernist shapes in tea sets, vases and a stunning range of cocktail shakers (Plate 6.28).

6.2 Mogens Ballin Danish pewter and brass jewellery casket c.1902,
w. 20cm. (Didier Antiques London)

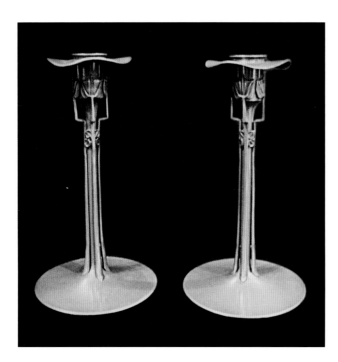

6.3 Santesson pewter candlesticks after a design by Archibald Knox. It is not
known whether these were an authorised use of the design originally produced
by Liberty & Co. in silver; they are nearly an exact reproduction in pewter.
1906, h. 26cm. (Titus Omega)

6.4 Schreuder & Olsson of Stockholm Swedish pewter lamp bass c.1905,
h. 41cm. (Bacchus Stockholm)

6.5 Schreuder & Olsson of Stockholm Swedish pewter candlesticks c.1905, h. 13cm. (Bacchus Stockholm)

6.6 Schreuder & Olsson of Stockholm Swedish pewter inkwell c.1905, w. 13cm. (Bacchus Stockholm)

6.7 Schreuder & Olsson of Stockholm Swedish pewter inkstand c.1905, w. 18cm. (Bacchus Stockholm)

6.8 Olof Ahlberg for Schreuder & Olsson of Stockholm. Swedish Art Nouveau pewter dish with fish and wave motif c.1904, d. 35 cm. (Photo B4 20ᵗʰ Century Design NYC)

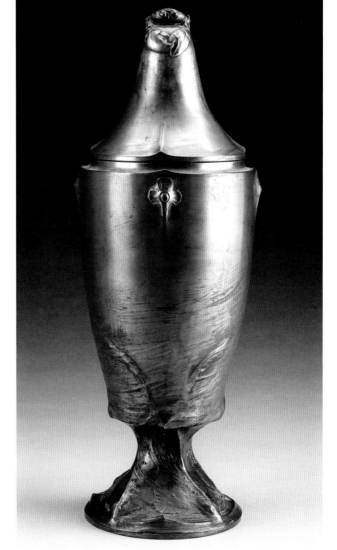

6.9 Schreuder & Olsson pewter lidded vase c.1904, h. 40cm. Marked 'Schreuder & Olsson Stockholm, Made in Sweden'. (Jacksons Stockholm)

6.11 Swedish pewter candelabra designed by C. Fagerbeg for
Herman Bergmann c.1910, h. 46 cm. (Photo:Jacksons Stockholm)

6.10 R. Busek for Schreuder & Olsson of Stockholm. Swedish pewter jug
c.1910, h. 25cm. (Photo: Sjöström Antik Stockholm)

6.12 Schreuder & Olsson of Stockholm pewter letter opener c.1904, l. 20cm.
(Bacchus Stockholm)

6.13 Svenskt Tenn pewter box designed by Nils Fougstedt c.1920s, h. 15cm,
d.11.5cm, w. 21.4cm. Stamped with Svenskt Tenns angelmark.
(Photo: Jacksons Stockholm)

6.14 Svenskt Tenn candlesticks designed by Anna Petrus 1920, h. 26.5cm. A pair of very rare pewter candlesticks with brass details. Stamped B1928. (Photo: Jacksons Stockholm)

6.15 Svenskt Tenn modernist candelabra designed by Nils Fougstedt c.1920s, h. 50cm. (Photo: Jacksons Stockholm)

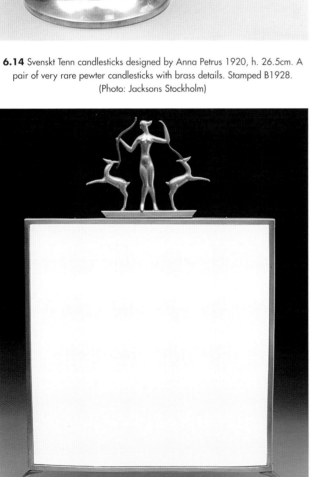

6.16 Svenskt Tenn mirror designed by Nils Fougstedt 1920, h. 60cm, w. 44cm. Frame in pewter and brass. Svenskt tenn and date stamps. (Photo: Jacksons Stockholm)

6.17 Svenskt Tenn modernist candelabra designed by Björn Trägårdh 1930,
h. 19.5cm, d. 32.5cm. Svenskt Tenn Angel mark and date stamp 'D-8' for
1930. (Photo: Jacksons Stockholm)

6.18 Svenskt Tenn modernist vase designed by Nils Fougstedt c.1920,
h. 26cm. Pewter and brass. (Photo: Jacksons Stockholm)

6.19 Svenskt Tenn Modernist vase designed by Nils Fougstedt c.1930,
h. 30cm. (Tony Victoria Gallery NYC)

6.21 Detail of Svenskt Tenn table by Uno Åhrén 1929, 300 x 110cm.
(Photo: Jacksons Stockholm)

6.20 Svenskt Tenn table and screen designed by Uno Åhrén for American
client Mrs Isabelle Clow. The pieces were the centrepiece of an exhibition held
at the National Museum, Stockholm in 1929. Both are fashioned in sheet
pewter with brass inlay. Screen: 333 x 90cm, table: 300 x 110cm.
(Photo: Jacksons Stockholm)

6.22 Modernist Svenskt Tenn bowl designed by Björn Trägårdh c.1930,
h.11.5cm, d. 33.5cm. Pewter and brass. Angel marks and date stamp 'D8' for
1930. Probably made for the Stockholm Exhibition, 1930.
(Photo: Jacksons Stockholm)

6.23 Svenskt Tenn pewter and brass vase c.1930, h. 22cm, d. 18.5cm. The designer is unknown, but the piece is similar in style to the furniture inlays of Uno Åhrén. (Photo: Jacksons Stockholm)

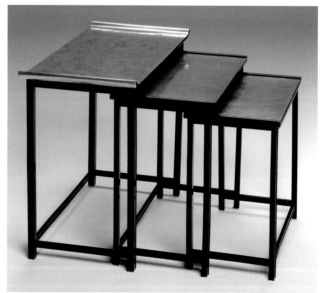

6.24 Svenskt Tenn nest of tables designed by Nils Fougstedt 1929, h. 56cm, d. 35cm, w. 64cm. Engraved pewter tops with decoration of Noah's Ark. Black stained bases. Top table with the Angel mark of Svenskt Tenn and date mark 'C8' for 1929. See also details of engraved panels (Plate 6.25). (Photo: Jacksons Stockholm)

6.25 Details of the panels in the Svenskt Tenn tables shown in Plate 6.24. All were designed by Nils Fougstedt, 1929. (Photos: Jacksons Stockholm)

6.26 Svenskt Tenn pewter and glass ceiling lamp designed by Anna Petrus c.1920, h. 96cm, d. 84cm. (Photo: Jacksons Stockholm)

6.28 GAB (Guldsmedsaktiebolaget) modernist cigarette box c.1930, h. 12cm. (FCR Gallery London)

6.27 Pewter-topped table designed by Nils Fougstedt c.1920, h. 61cm, d. 72cm. Pewter top with engraved figures and black lacquered base. (Photo: Jacksons Stockholm)

6.29 Modernst pewter vase designed by Sylvia Stave for Hallberg c.1930, h. 20cm. (FCR Gallery London)

6.30 Modernst pewter vase with handles on ebony base designed by Sylvia Stave for Hallberg c.1930, h. 22cm. (FCR Gallery London)

6.31 Just Andersen Disko double candelabra, 1930s. Stamped 'Just' in triangle, '1660', h. 11.5cm, w. 19cm. (Photo: Freeforms NYC)

6.32 Just Andersen, Denmark, pair of Disko metal candelabra c.1930s, h. 22cm, w. 25cm. Impressed 'Danmark', 'Just', '819'. (Photo: Freeforms NYC)

6.34 Just Andersen, Denmark, Disko footed vase, 1930s, h. 24cm, w. 20cm. Stamped 'Danmark', 'Just' in triangle, '1249'. (Photo: Freeforms NYC)

6.33 Just Andersen Disko candelabra, 1930s. Stamped 'Just' in triangle, 'Disko metal 74', h. 22cm, w. 18cm. (Photo: Freeforms NYC)

6.35 Just Andersen Disko metal candelabrum (model 1124) c.1930, w. 39cm, h. 29cm. (Private Collection London)

6.36 Just Andersen, Denmark, pair of Disko vases, c. 1930s, h. 20cm, w. 14cm. Stamped 'Just' and '1925' (Photo: Freeforms NYC)

6.38 Just Andersen, Denmark, Disko ribbed vase c. 1920s-30s, h. 13.5cm, w. 10cm. Stamped 'Danmark', 'Just' triangle monogram, 'D2479'. (Photo: Freeforms NYC)

6.37 Just Andersen, Denmark, pair of bookends with mermaid figures in Disko metal, 1930s, h. 12cm, w. 11.5cm. Impressed 'JUST' in triangle, '1554'. (Photo: Freeforms NYC)

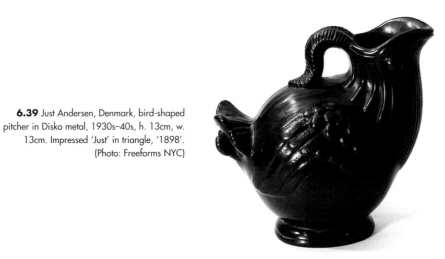

6.39 Just Andersen, Denmark, bird-shaped pitcher in Disko metal, 1930s–40s, h. 13cm, w. 13cm. Impressed 'Just' in triangle, '1898'. (Photo: Freeforms NYC)

6.40 Just Andersen, Denmark, open-mouthed fish vessel in Disko metal, c.1930s–40s, h. 9.5cm, w. 13cm. Impressed 'Just' in triangle, '1389'. (Freeforms NYC)

6.41 Just Andersen, Denmark. Disko metal, c.1930s–40s, h. 15 cm. (Freeforms NYC)

Examples of Makers' Marks

AMERICAN PEWTER

The Aesthetic and Art Nouveau movements were enthusiastically embraced by America. The 1876 Philadelphia Centennial Exhibition inspired a new generation of designers and painters with their elaborate Japanese display. These young designers assimilated these international styles into their visual lexicon, adding their own individual embellishments along the way. In the area of decorative arts, Louis Comfort Tiffany (1848-1933) was perhaps the best know advocate with his magnificent use of bronze and glass. Metal objects made by Tiffany Studios of New York were retailed in Europe through Bing in Paris. They were featured in *Studio* magazine in England, influencing a generation of craftsmen. Tiffany was seminal in promoting his own form of the Aesthetic movement with the company's Japonisme, Persian and native American detailing; this is evident in the diverse range of metalware which was

produced for the desk and table. Most items were fashioned in bronze then patinated with gold or various antique finishes (Plate 7.1). The clientele for Tiffany Studios shared a similar visual sophistication to the patrons of Liberty & Co. and Morris & Co. in England, as well as Samuel Bing's emporium, L'Art Nouveau, in Paris. Luxurious items in silver and bronze were expensive and time-consuming to manufacture. A cost effective solution was recognised by utilising pewter or Britannia metal and modern moulding technology as an alternative.

Gorham

Gorham, founded in 1865 and located in Providence, Rhode Island, was a celebrated company best known for their exclusive range of silver and mixed metal cabinet pieces. Gorham espoused and promoted both the Aesthetic movement and the Art Nouveau style by

7.1 Tiffany gilt bronze desk set with owl design inspired by native American handicraft c.1905-1910, pen tray l. 23cm. (FCR Gallery London)

creating the Martele range of hand-crafted silver objects. This exclusive line was overseen by William C. Codman, an English designer/craftsman. The range was extremely expensive and laborious to produce, but fortunately the investment paid off and Gorham were internationally celebrated at the 1900 Exposition Universelle in Paris where they received five gold medals. This acknowledgment raised the profile of Gorham, who continued to mass produce a more commercial and affordable Britannia metal range. Some of Gorham's Britannia items were in the Art Nouveau style, incorporating naturalistic elements such as insects flowers and shells into the designs.

American Arts & Crafts Pewter

Pewter was also making its way into the exhibitions and showrooms of the smaller Arts & Crafts workshops springing up around America. The revival of pewter as a medium was sparked by a renewed interest in this material as it filtered over from Europe. Pewter was also widely used in eighteenth- and early nineteenth-century America for domestic items such as plates and tankards, so it wasn't entirely surprising that pewter had a resurgence in the new century.

Karl Kipp was one of the founders of The Roycrofters, a reformist community of craft workers located in East Aurora, New York. He began his career as a bookbinder, but soon moved into the production of hammered copper and pewterware. Around 1895-1903, Kipp produced a number of pewter items including trays, vases and drinking sets (Plate 7.15). The furniture maker Gustav Stickley was also aware of the revival of handcraftsmanship in England when he spearheaded what became known as the 'Mission' style in America. Some fine examples of Stickley furniture designed by Harvey Ellis incorporate inlaid pewter in the manner of H. Ballie Scott and the Guild Of Handicrafts into decorative panels adorning the backs of chairs and the doors of cabinets (Plate 7.11). Small workshops had also begun to produce items in pewter, echoing the fashion for hand-crafted luxury items.

Rebecca Cauman

Boston metal-smith Rebecca Cauman (born 1872) produced beautifully crafted enamelled bowls and was especially known for her covered boxes, many of which

had enamelled interiors. Rebecca attended the Massachusetts College of Art and the Rhode Island School of Design (Plate 7.16). Her Pewter items had an elegant simplicity – they were similar to her production in silver and copper, but with added copper and enamelled cabochons.

After the First World War, many of the larger American factories reproduced the look of handplanished pewter. This popular style remained fervent throughout the 1920s.

Serge Nekrassoff

Serge Nekrassoff was born in Russia, in 1895. He served in the Russian Imperial Guard and, like many, was forced to emigrate at the time of the Russian Revolution. In 1919 he became an apprentice metalworker in Paris, with copper being his most common medium. Nekrassoff moved to New York around 1925 and opened his first workshop on 14th Street. It was at this point that he began producing work in pewter. In the 1930s Nekrassoff relocated to Darien, Connecticut, where he expanded his workshop and employed up to 18 craftsmen. He developed a house style which is somewhat reminiscent of Georg Jensen, incorporating stylised floral motifs and hand-planished surface decoration.[1]

Meriden

The Meriden Britannia Company of Meriden, Connecticut, founded in 1869, was one of America's most proficient makers of fine silver-plated pewter/ Britannia metal. Some of the items were finished with a planished surface echoing items made by Liberty & Co. in England.

7.2 Meriden Britannia Co. Factory 1899.

1. Dr. Henry Gans, Maine Antique Digest 2002.

7.3 A Meriden Aesthetic movement Britannia metal tea set with oriental-style decoration. (Illustration from the 1900 Meriden catalogue)

7.4 Meriden Aesthetic movement vases with oriental-style decoration. Illustration from the1900 Meriden catalogue.

7.5 Meriden pewter chamberstick fashioned as a grouse claw and acorn c.1890, h. 12cm. (Private Collection Boston)

7.6 Meriden pewter sweetmeats tray c.1905, l. 20cm. (FCR Gallery London)

7.7 Meriden pewter figural napkin ring fashioned as a boy rolling a barrel c.1900, h. 8cm. (FCR Gallery London)

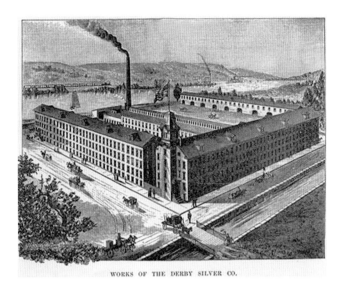

WORKS OF THE DERBY SILVER CO.

7.8 The Derby Silver Co., Shelton, Connecticut, 1897.

7.9 Derby Silver Co. silver-plated pewter champagne cooler c.1905, h. 26cm. (FCR Gallery London)

The Derby Silver Co.

The Derby Silver Co., founded 1872 in Shelton Connecticut, produced a varied range of flat and hollow-ware which was sold through their own retail outlets in New York City, Chicago and San Francisco. Items such as the champagne cooler (Plate 7.9) in a conservative but stylish Art Nouveau style with a sinuous floral design, were typical of this factories quality and sophistication. Some of Derby's items were stamped 'Victor Silver Plate Company'. This was most likely Derby's budget range of goods sold through the S & H (Sperry and Hutchinson) green stamp outlets.[2]

The International Silver Company

The International Silver Company, founded in 1898, can trace its origins to Ashbil Griswold, an entrepreneur who established a pewter workshop in Meriden, Connecticut, in 1808 (see above).

Around the turn of the twentieth century, thirteen workshops and factories, including the Manhattan Silverplate Company, Rogers Brothers of Waterbury Connecticut, Meriden, Derby, Webster and Wilcox merged into the International Silver Company. This strengthened the finances of all of the companies involved and secured the future of these smaller factories.

They all produced a similar range of cutlery and hollow-ware based on traditional Sheffield designs. A few experimental items in the Art Nouveau style were produced, including a lamp by Webster (Plate 7.14), however most lacked the imagination and fluidly of their European counterparts such as Germany's WMF. It is possible that the merger of these companies led to a conservative backlash from centralised management directives as most of the examples of pewter that I have found are either based on traditional American shapes, such as the designs of Paul Revere, and popular traditional models similar to those available in English pattern books of the period.

Pairpoint

Pairpoint was another factory located on the East coast of America in New Bedford, Massachusetts. It began as the Mount Washington Glass Company in 1894, later merging with a small local Britannia metal workshop to form the Pairpoint Manufacturing Company. They received encouraging praise for their designs for lamps and tableware, including tea sets and candlesticks. In 1900 Pairpoint became the Pairpoint Corporation. This

2. www.derbyhistorical.org

HUNTRESS BALL SWING
1901

7.10a Ansonia swing clock illustration from the 1900 Ansonia catalogue.

7.10b Ansonia pewter Art Nouveau mantle clock with bronze patination c.1900, h. 41cm. This clock shows a strong European influence. (Photo: O'Gallerie, Portland)

7.11 Detail of pewter inlay work on a side chair designed by Harvey Ellis for Gustav Stickley c.1903. (Private Collection Boston)

company is best known for their reverse painted lamps with unusual pewter bases, some fashioned as animals and tree trunks. Another example of Pairpoint's inventiveness is clearly seen in the novelty cigar compendium designed as a champagne bottle. All of the sections unscrew to reveal an ashtray cigar compartment and match holder (Plate 7.18).

The Ansonia Clock Manufacturing Company

The Ansonia Clock Manufacturing Company of New York produced elaborate ormolu designs in Britannia metal with gilded figures. Later on in the early 1900s they produced a number of designs in the continental Art Nouveau style. Many of the clocks have figural maidens in sensual poses.

Art Deco and Beyond

After the First World War, some interesting designs in pewter emerged in the Modernist and Art Deco styles. American pewter for the most part remained conservative and traditional, however there are a few examples that merit mention such as, the Cubist tea-set, 'Diament', designed by Gene Theobald and Virginia Hamill c.1930 for the Wilcox Silverplate Company. This

was manufactured in silver plated Britannia metal with Bakelite handles and utilised ocean liner style stream-lining to create a compact set that fitted together on the tray like a sculptural puzzle (Plate 7.20). The smokers' compendium by Josef Hoffmann's son, Wolfgang, employs a Modernist approach to design in the Bauhaus style which is particularly successful (Plate 7.22).

Many novelty cocktail shakers were produced during this period, including the 'Golf Bag' designed by G. H. Berry in 1926. It was manufactured by the Derby Silver Company in Britannia metal and has the distinction of being one of the earliest novelty cocktail shakers produced. Also of note were the designs produced in the 1930s for bookends, match holders and bowls from Russel Wright; many bring into play animal forms.

7.12 A Pairpoint 'puffy' glass lampshade on an ornate Britannia metal base, c.1900, h. 41 cm. The shade is signed 'The Pairpoint Corp.' and the base is marked with the diamond 'PP' on the bottom. (Photo: The Antique Traders, San Francisco)

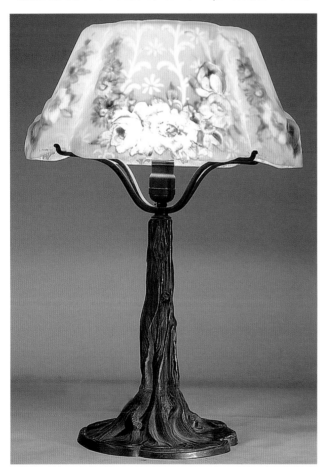

7.13 A Pairpoint Art Nouveau reverse-painted 'puffy' frosted glass lampshade on a bronze patinated pewter 'tree-trunk' base, c.1900, h. 59cm, signed 'Pairpoint Corp.'. (Photo: The Antique Traders, San Francisco)

7.14 E. G. Webster & Son pewter Art Nouveau lamp in the continental style c.1910, h. 51cm. (Photo: Rick Kaplan Antiques)

7.15 Karl Kipp American Arts & Crafts pewter beaker c.1919, h. 13cm. (Private Collection Boston)

7.16 Rebecca Cauman pewter trinket box with copper enamel cabochon c.1910, h. 10cm. (Chicago Silver)

7.17 The 'Golf Bag' designed by G. H. Berry in 1926, h. 31cm. Manufactured by the Derby Silver Company in Britannia metal. (Photo Mark Bigler Utah)

7.18 Pairpoint Art Deco novelty cigar compendium fashioned as a champagne bottle c.1920, h. 26cm. (FCR Gallery London)

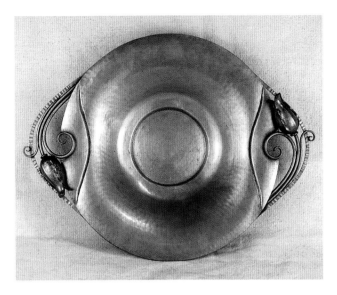

7.19 Serge Nekrassoff hand-hammered pewter bowl with stylised tulip motif c.1930, w. 39cm. (Photo: Vincent Imondi)

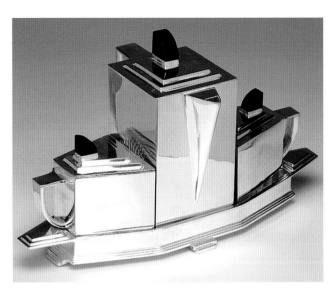

7.20 Wilcox Silverplate Co. Modernist 'Diamante' tea set made of Britannia metal with Bakelite handles designed by Gene Theobald and Virginia Hamill c.1930. (Private Collection Canada)

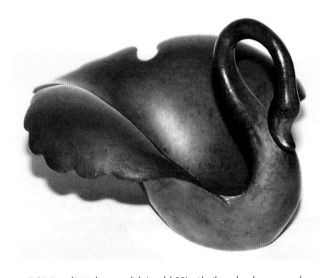

7.21 Russel Wright swan dish (model 30) with silver-plated pewter on the bottom, c.1930, d. 9cm. (Sidekikz' Vintage Collectibles)

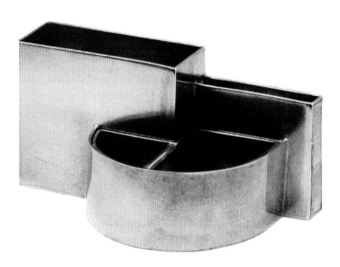

7.22 Pewter smoker's compendium designed by Wolfgang Hoffmann for the Early American Pewter Company c.1930, l. 20cm. (Photo Ellis Nadler)

Examples of Makers' Marks

JAPAN

Dr Christopher Dresser, the botanist and designer, visited Japan as the invited guest of the Emperor in1876. He was the first designer and one of a very select elite of foreigners to be allowed access to what was then a closed society. He was presented with a large collection of domestic items, mainly ceramics, that are now housed in the Victoria & Albert Museum in London. At the same time, Dresser presented Japan with a collection of British ceramics. This important exchange of everyday household objects had a lasting effect on international design in the twentieth century.

Liberty & Co. commissioned a number of items in silver by Konoike of Yokohama. Objects for serving tea, including spoons and a tea pot with chased chrysanthemums now housed in the V & A. The items have English import marks for 1896-1897.[1]

There is little information available on pewter production in Japan in the first part of the century, however there is a page in the 1902 Liberty Yuletide Catalogue which illustrates examples of Japanese antimony-ware sold in the Bazaar section of Liberty's emporium around 1900. The pewter items are varied, many with bronze patination to mimic Japanese bronzes which were popular during the period. The objects were made for export and reflect the British taste. Depictions of Dresser-style frogs in the form of candlesticks are playful and humorous (Plate 8.2). Photo frames with coin-like medallions of geishas and useful boxes for pins, stamps and matches are described as 'artistic designs in relief highly finished workmanship' and 'quaint artistic and well finished castings'.

8.1 Page from the 1901 Liberty catalogue describing their range of Japanese antimony-ware.

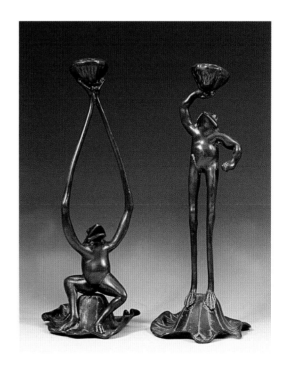

8.2 Pair of Japanese Aesthetic Movement antimony-ware bronze patinated frog candlesticks retailed through Liberty & Co. c.1900, h. 30cm.
(FCR Gallery London)

1. *Liberty: Masters Of Style & Decoration* by Stephen Calloway p. 89.

8.3 A Japanese Aesthetic Movement antimony-ware silver plated frog candlestick retailed through Liberty & Co. c.1900, h. 30cm. (FCR Gallery London)

8.4 A Japanese Art Nouveau antimony-ware silver plated photo frame c.1910, h. 18cm, marked 'Japan' on reverse. (FCR Gallery London)

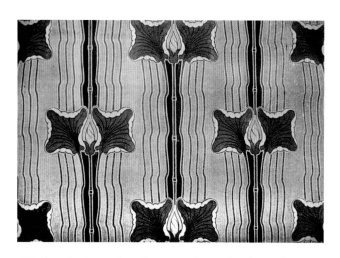

8.5 Christopher Dresser design for cretonne showing the influence of Japanese design. (Photo: *The Studio*, 1900

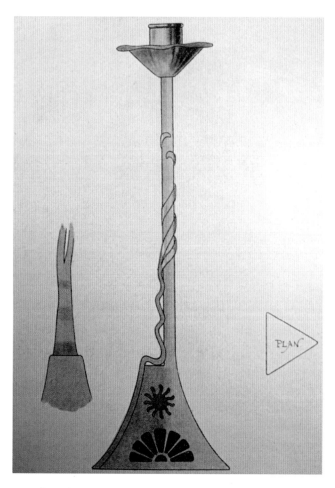

8.6 Christopher Dresser candlestick design showing the influence of Japanese design. (Photo: *The Studio*, 1900)

PEWTER RESTORATION

Doros Charalambides explains the process of cleaning and polishing pewter

Doros Charalambides is a second-generation restorer of pewter and an expert in the area of 20th century pewter. His workshop Red Bus Restorations (formally Andrews) is located in North London.

> The process of stripping and preparing pewter is hazardous. It should _always_ be executed by a professional and _never_ attempted at home. The following information is included in the book for interest only.

Preparation and Stripping

1. Before work begins, it must be ascertained that the material is actually pewter. The following points are considered:

  * Which metals have been combined to form the alloy
  * Whether the piece is silver- or chromium-plated
  * How many moulded pieces make up the object

Once this has been established, the item can be stripped.

2. Stripping the pewter back to the base metal is carried out by submerging the item in a special combination of acids. This is done twice: once to remove the layer of silver plate, following which the item is rinsed, and then a second time, so as to soften and clean the item.

3. The item is cleaned using a scratch brush, or fine brass brush, with water.

4. Next, the expert can perform any aspects of restoration on the item, such as straightening, soldering and removing dents.

Polishing

1. The first process is called satine and uses a grit-based adhesive. This polish dries hard on a cloth-based mop and, when applied to the pewter item, it removes all of the scratches to achieve a matt finish. The dressing used comes in various grades from rough, for bad pitting, to smooth for an even finish. This is a tricky procedure and if it is done incorrectly, maker's marks and delicate decoration can be removed accidentally.

2. Recarving of decoration. For this, mops, sandpaper and various cutting tools are needed. Application of this technique provides crispness and can only be correctly executed by a qualified artist/craftsman.

3. Varying grades of polishing stitch mops and a compound mix of abrasions and petroleum grease are used to give the item lustre.

4. A high glass finish is achieved by polishing the item, first on a machine, and then by hand to reach any smaller or more intricate areas.

5. The hyfin process is named after the white abrasive used for this stage. The hyfin is applied to the item using an open mop made from rough cotton. This adds sheen to the piece.

Cleaning

Once the items have been polished, they must also be degreased. After this, they are once more scratch brushed, this time with a soft bristle mop and water. Then they are rinsed and dried.

Finishing

This is carried out using a soft cloth mop, paraffin, and jeweller's rouge. They are applied with a brush mop and buffed to achieve a mirror finish.

PEWTER AFTERCARE

There are two schools of thought in reference to the cleaning of 20th century pewter. Conventionally, antique pewter is not stripped of its patina, as this will severely devalue the object, but 20th century pewter must be assessed differently. The key purpose for developing Britannia metal was for use as a base metal for silver plating. It was marketed and sold as an alternative to silver, or 'poor man's silver'. As many collectors of traditional pewter move into the 20th century market, they convey their previous conceptions of what pewter should look like onto this area of collecting.

The author is of the opinion that 20th century pewter should be restored to its former glory and that means that it should be polished until it has a mirror finish. In my capacity as a dealer, I am often asked how I get my pewter so bright. Collectors also often ask how to maintain pewter that has been professionally polished.

It is a simple process and it takes much less care and effort then silver. 20th century pewter contains a small amount of silver and this polishes up to give pieces a fine lustre. It is important to use a good quality chromium paste polish and these are available from any automotive care shop.

1. Use a small dab of paste and apply it with a soft rag or old t-shirt in a circular motion. The t-shirt will blacken as the oxidation is removed.
2. Repeat if necessary and rinse with warm water and washing up liquid.
3. Dry and polish with a clean soft cloth.
4. Use impregnated silver polishing mitts to remove fingerprints and maintain a shine.

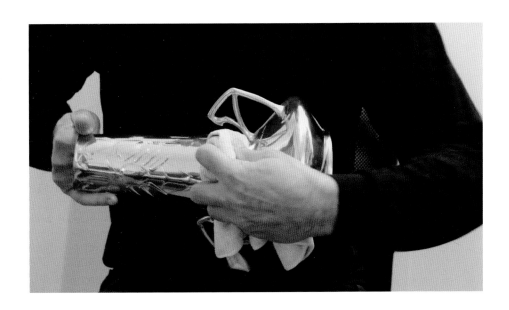

REPRODUCTIONS

A reproduction is defined in the Oxford English Dictionary as being 'made to imitate the style of an earlier period or particular craftsman'. A reproduction is not made to outwardly deceive the buyer. However, a reproduction in the hands of the unscrupulous can be altered and passed off as the genuine article. Hence, the expression 'caveat emptor' or 'let the buyer beware' is always a sensible approach to take when buying antiques. It is important to recognise that most twentieth-century pewter of note has a set market value determined by the hundreds of items sold at auction and by dealers each year.

These are the golden questions to apply when buying pewter:

1) Step back and look at the condition of the item – does it look 100 years old?
2) Has the item has been professionally polished, re-plated and patinated?
3) Do the marks seem correct?

4) Does the weight feel right? Is it too light or too heavy?
5) Why is the item so inexpensive/expensive?

There have been numerous reproductions of Art Nouveau and Arts and Crafts pewter available on the market since the 1960s.

The best of these are the WMF models made in Italy by the Cosi Tabellini Company in Brescia. The composition of the alloy used is 93% tin, 5% antimony, and 2% copper.[1] There are thirty or so models which tend to be a little heavier than the originals, but they are surprisingly well crafted. These modern reproductions do not bear the WMF markings but instead have the angel mark of Achille Gamba, one of Cosi Tabellini's brand names. Sometimes these are also marked with 'etain 95%' (see page 228). This range of pewter is available to buy in many international antiques markets. The range is also sold in museum shops and department stores.

Liberty & Co. reissued a number of pewter items in the late 1990s, including several of the popular Knox designs of candlesticks, vases and bowls. These bear the mark 'Liberty Heritage'. They also retailed many reproduction pewter designs, such as Kayserzinn and a reissue of the J. M. Olbrich twin branch candelabrum (Plate 1.193).

Another company resurrecting the Kayserzinn name has also surfaced, producing a number of reissues of vases, bowls and candlesticks. They are marked using a smaller logo and the numbers do not always correspond to the originals used at the turn of the century.

There are many other reproductions on the market, including a crude range of Knox-inspired designs which are a poor pastiche of his clocks, boxes and photo frames. These are cold-enamelled and bear little resemblance to the originals.

I have also found poor examples of the well known Orivit maiden candelabrum (Plate 1.108). These are often mounted on onyx bases and have an applied bronze patination.

Most of the reproductions mentioned are of a reasonable quality both in the moulding and in the finishing. There are also items produced in the 1960s-1970s which have aged naturally and look quite authentic. This will always create a challenge for the novice collector as well as the serious buyer of twentieth-century pewter.

1. (osi Tabellini, www.artofpewter.it

Examples of Reproduction Marks

Bibliography

Art Nouveau Domestic Metalwork from WMF (book of the 1906 catalogue), Antique Collectors' Club 1988

Arwas, Victor, *Liberty Style*, Arco 1983

Billcliffe, Roger, *Charles Rennie Mackintosh: The Complete Furniture, Furniture Drawings & Interior Designs*, Lutterworth Press 1979

Bloom-Heisinger, Kathryn, *Art Nouveau in Munich: Masters of Jugendstil*, Philadelphia Museum of Art 1988

Burschell, Carlo and Heinz Scheiffele, *WMF Ikora Metall/Metalwork*, Arnoldsche 2006

Calloway, Stephen, *Liberty of London: Masters of Style & Decoration*, Thames & Hudson 1992

Collecting by Design: Silver and Metalwork of the Twentieth Century, Margo Grant Walsh Collection, Museum of Fine Arts Houston, Yale University Press, 2008

Couldrey, Vivienne, *The Art of Louis Comfort Tiffany*, Quarto 1989

Curtis, Tony, *Lyle Price Guide Art Nouveau & Deco*, Lyle 1992

Dahhan, Philippe, *Étains 1900: 200 sculpteurs de la Belle Epoque*, Les Editions de l'Amateur 2000

Duncan, Alastair, *The Paris Salons 1895-1914*, vol. V: 'Objets d'Art & Metalware', Antique Collectors' Club 1999

Drucker, Janet, *Georg Jensen*, Schiffer 1997

English Pewter Designed and Made by Liberty & Co. (catalogue), c.1920

Fahr-Becker, Gabriele, *Wiener Werkstätte 1903-1932*, Taschen 1995

Groot, Leidelmeijer & Eiléns (eds), *Avant-Garde Design: Dutch Decorative Arts 1880-1940*, Philip Wilson 1997

J P Kayser Sohn Krefeld Musterbuch 1907 (catalogue)

Kwint, Jab C. G., *Urania Maastricht 1903-1910*, V&K Publishing 2002

Leonhardt, Zülsdorff and Götz, *Friedrich Adler*, Arnoldsche 1994

Levy, Mervyn, *Liberty Style: The Classic Years 1898-1910*, Rizzoli 1986

Liberty Style (catalogue for touring exhibition Japan), 1999

Liberty Yuletide Catalogue, 1909

Lyons, Harry, *Christopher Dresser the People's Designer 1834-1904*, Antique Collectors' Club 2005

Martin, Stephen A., *Archibald Knox*, Artmedia 1988

Miller, Judith, *Arts & Crafts*, Dorling Kindersley 2004

Miller's Art Nouveau & Art Deco Buyer's Guide 1995

Modern Art of Metalwork, Brohan Museum catalogue 1990

Morris, Barbara, *Liberty Design*, Pyramid 1989

Ricke, Vicek, Adlerova & Ploill, *Lotz Bohmisches Glas 1880-1940 Band I & II*, Prestel-Verlag 1989

Schuster, Peter-Klaus, *Peter Behrens und Nürnberg*, Prestel 1980

Silzer, Sammlung Giorgio, *Erlesenes aus Jugendstil und Art Deco*, Passage-Verlag 1997

Stara, Dagmar, *Guide to Pewter Marks of the World*, Aventinum 1977

Studio, The, 1900-1910

Tilbrook, Adrian J., *The Designs of Archibald Knox for Liberty & Co.*, Ornament Press 1976

Vaupel, Elisabeth, *Orivit Zinn des Jugenstils aus Koln*, Kölnisches Stadt Museum, 1991

Weisberg, Gabriel P., *Art Nouveau Bing Paris Style 1900*, Abrams 1986

Index